An Early
Journey Home

An Early Journey Home

Helping Dying Children and Grieving Families

Mary Ann Froehlich

*A book for anyone who has known
or will know loss . . . EVERYONE*

BAKER BOOK HOUSE
Grand Rapids, Michigan 49516

ISBN: 0-8010-3561-9

Printed in the United States of America

Dedicated to all those children
who have taken an early journey home
and the families
who remained behind.

With deep appreciation to the families
who have shared their experiences.
Names have often been changed
to protect their privacy.

Acknowledgments

I want to thank those who shared the vision for this book and offered their expertise to bring it to completion: Steve Fretwell; John Froehlich; Rev. Gerald Hill; Virginia Hiramatsu; the team at Baker Book House; David Wiersbe; and dear friends who prayed for this project.

I am especially grateful to those families who shared their grief experiences: Victoria and Mike Haskins, Virginia and Ron Hiramatsu, Don Matlock, Doral and Diana Matlock, Carol and Fred Patterson, Kathy and David Werum, and many families who chose to remain anonymous.

Contents

Contents

1

An Early Journey Home

Kim expired. Sunday 10:45 A.M."

Expired? I stared at the message posted at the therapist's center. It was Monday morning, and Kim had died almost a full twenty-four hours before.

Expired? What an odd word to use. Was the technical aspect of *expiration* supposed to distance us from the intense pain of Kim's death?

Expired? No, Kim had died and gone before us to take an early journey home.

I had been working at Children's Hospital only a couple of months when Kim became my first "favorite patient." She was a shy, blonde, blue-eyed, seven-year-old girl with leukemia, who was afraid of most of the hospital staff. She had opened up to me easily during our music therapy sessions and began to ask for me daily whenever she was hospitalized. It was easy for me to become attached to her; ours was a mutual love affair.

Medically Kim was not supposed to die. She had a type of leukemia that was treatable, and she had been doing well at home in remission. But that Sunday morning she came to the hospital slumped over her father's shoulder and could not be revived.

Kim's funeral was the first child's funeral I had ever attended. The strongest memory that remains with me is the mental picture of her thirteen-year-old sister, who had been inseparable from Kim, crying uncontrollably at the graveside and her parents trying to comfort her in the midst of their own grief. I knew that the pain they felt would gradually decrease in intensity but always be with them.

I am not an expert on the death of a child. An expert is someone who has walked the road before. I am no expert, because I have not personally lost one of my own children. People like Kim's parents are experts.

I have stood by to help many dying children and shared the grief of the families who have lost them. Yet I know now my deep pain and loss did not even come close to their suffering.

Saying good-bye to one's own child is the most painful of human experiences. The parents travel the hardest journey. This book is not written for them, however. It is written for helpers who desire to effectively minister to hospitalized and terminally ill children and share the burden of loss with their families. It is a task that will exhaust such helpers physically, emotionally, mentally, and spiritually.

Death and grief are well-studied topics in secular and Christian circles. Yet the loss of a child is an area that some of us Christians still shy away from. It strikes too close to the core of our faith. It brings too many questions. Yet I believe that the majority of today's Christians want to deal with this tougher issue. You are one of them or you would not be reading this book.

If we can learn to minister to persons who suffer this deepest, painful loss, we will be better equipped to help anyone who grieves a loss. This book is written for pastors, chaplains, Christian health-care professionals, lay ministers, and friends of suffering families. Part 1 lays a biblical foundation to prepare the helper. Part 2 is about helping the dying child. Part 3 is about helping the grieving family. Part 4 lists resources and tools for helping.

I did not write this book alone. God wrote this book through many special families who courageously shared their stories with me. Each did so with great anguish and tears. We often cried together. And why did these families endure this pain? For *you*. Their answer was always the same: "If I can help someone else live through this, I want to do it."

I interviewed the majority of the families and asked a few to write their own stories. Some requested to remain anonymous. All the grievers said it was a very painful but therapeutic process to relive their stories, and it brought further closure to the most painful experiences of their lives.

No human being escapes facing one's own death and the death of one's loved ones. It is life's eventual certainty. We must all take the journey.

2

My Own Journey

My dear friend and co-worker warned me that I was getting too close to Julie. Julie was a fragile six-year-old girl dying of cystic fibrosis. Struggling to make ends meet financially, her parents could rarely visit her. I spent every minute possible with Julie when she was hospitalized. She was usually found sitting on my lap or being carried by me through the hospital. I even attended her birthday party at the family's mobile home park and remember that we couldn't light the candles on her birthday cake because of her oxygen tank. I had never been so attached to a patient. Her slow, lingering death hit me very hard. I accepted her death, but I would constantly ask God why she had to suffer so terribly.

My greatest weakness as a therapist was that I could not distance myself from the patients the way my co-workers could. Not yet having children of my own, the patients became "my" children. This intimacy forced me to take my own journey of pain and questions.

If you commit yourself to helping dying children and their families, you, too, will have to take a personal journey in the process. I share my experiences with you to help prepare you for the obstacles ahead.

As the months passed into years, the deaths of patients began to blur together in my mind, but my memories of them still haunted me. Tina was a spunky six-year-old who was dying of leukemia and fighting it all the way. Tina was also a ham, and our music sessions were a great success. We made tapes together singing her original compositions. We even taped a video in the hospital filming department. She played every instrument and sang every song that we could think of. We then had a screening in her hospital room, attended by her doctors, nurses, family, and friends. She had always dreamed of being a TV star and now she was. Tina was bright, talented, pretty, and dying.

At her memorial service, to my shock and surprise, the minister played one of our tapes. I had no preparation for that moment, and it was too painful to hear that small voice singing again after her death.

Tony was an eighteen-year-old Down syndrome young man who went into a coma and died following heart surgery. His mother, who never left his side, was devastated. As I later related this experience to friends, they would ignorantly suggest that perhaps "his death was a blessing since he was disabled." Anyone who has known or worked with Down syndrome individuals knows that they are some of the most precious, giving people that God has placed on this earth. Tony was his mother's son and had been the focus of her life for eighteen years. The hole that was left after his death was unfillable. Not only did she need to deal with her own grief but she found a lack of sincere empathy from those around her.

I remember Charlie's mom coming often to the hospital after his death, bringing his toys and games to donate to the playroom. Charlie's mom was a single parent who had devoted her entire life to caring for her only child. When she lost Charlie, she lost her role in life as well. She lost her hospital lifeline. She had nowhere to go.

Erin was a two-year-old dying of a brain tumor. Her mother didn't want to miss one minute with her, so they slept together at night. I always wondered what that first night after Erin's death was like without that little body beside her.

Never to be documented in any textbook, I have observed one common characteristic in the dying children I've known. They seem to have a maturity and compassion for others far beyond their years. They are happy, giving, and courageous children. It is as if God has "grown them up" early for their special calling. You may be surprised to learn that a children's hospital can be a joyous place with more laughter than tears. Children are better equipped than adults to face death, for one reason: Children know how to live life to the fullest today and not focus on the lost future. Entering into this last celebration of life is the key to effectively helping dying children and their families.

There will be no way to diminish our grief upon the child's death. The price of intimacy is pain. Whenever we involve ourselves deeply in a relationship, we risk the pain of losing that loved one. That person has become a part of us, and it hurts when that part is cut away. It is no wonder that the most intimate of human relationships—parent to child—causes the greatest pain when it is severed. The process is major surgery and leaves a deep scar. Scratches heal and disappear. Scars heal and remain for life as reminders of past wounds. The initial pain may be gone, but the memory stays. The helper's scars are not as deep as the parents', but certainly they exist.

The greatest struggles on my journey to becoming an effective helper surprisingly did not come from the dying children and their families but from fellow Christians.

Most Christians, who are otherwise solidly grounded in their faith, are uncomfortable discussing or even thinking about dying children. Most doctrinal positions and theological beliefs do not prepare us for this tenderest aspect of human suffering.

Two specific experiences affected me during this time. The first occurred while I sat in church one Sunday morning lost in thought over a patient who had died the preceding Friday. In stark contrast, the head of the women's Bible group was announcing their next activity to be a tea where women could have "their fashion style and colors done."

It struck me with searing intensity that people were hurting and dying while the women of our church gave fashion classes. Where had the church lost sight of its real purpose, which is to be in the trenches of life with hurting people? The fact that the Christian life never was intended to be comfortable became undeniably real to me that Sunday morning.

The second experience occurred years before when I was a new Christian and in college. With some dear friends I became involved with the "God-intends-healing-wealth-and-success-for-his-people" movement. We were all healthy, vibrant young people interested in professional ministry as we embarked on life's adventure. I was seduced by the attractive philosophy as well. It wasn't that death and suffering were foreign to me. On the contrary, I had lost my share of dear relatives to heart attacks, cancer, and accidents. But since these tragedies happened to our family of non-Christians, it occurred to me that perhaps a life with God's care would prevent such painful experiences.

It wasn't long before my friend's husband developed a serious intestinal condition and lay dying in the hospital. The members of the group did not come to the hospital to visit, did not offer financial help, did not bring meals to his wife, or help in any other way. Instead they questioned the couple's faith, thereby adding guilt to their burden, and abandoned them. These Christians did not know how to suffer, and because of that fact did not know how to help the suffering. It scared them, paralyzed them, and incapacitated them for ministry. If the essence of the gospel was to equip the saints for ministry, then, as became clear to me, this view of Christianity was distorted and dangerous. It was a theology of spiritual immaturity.

My journey of experiences forced me to carefully study Scripture to grasp God's biblical answers about suffering and death, while I focused on children. Those discoveries I share with you in part 1 of this book.

PART 1

The Biblical Journey: Preparing the Helper

God is the ultimate expert. Other grieving parents are experts. But we are not experts; we are helpers. We are to stand by to love and uphold the grieving heart. For us to merely try to give advice to the dying child and the family is analogous to the nonswimmer standing on the shore yelling instructions at the swimmer caught in a riptide out in the ocean. If you can't dive into the water yourself and help carry the drowning swimmer out, then you are not the person to help. Helpers must be willing to enter the grieving process *with* the sufferers, not stand on the sidelines giving advice *to* the sufferers. Not only is advice giving not helpful; it can actually do harm. Jesus Christ calls us to be comforters, those who come alongside (paracletes). We are his ambassadors.

The purpose of this section is to offer a spiritual perspective on suffering and death to help you solidify your own spiritual foundation and relationship with God for the crises ahead. If you are floundering in your own sea of doubts when a child dies, you will be paralyzed and unable to help. This section is not intended as advice to be given to the grievers. Down the road you will be able to explore these biblical truths as *fellow grievers* searching for answers together, but that process is one of supporting each other and bearing one another's burdens, not of advice giving.

3

Helpers Without Answers

*Look, by reason of his power God is
     supreme,
     what teacher can be compared with
     him?
Who has ever told him which course to
     take,
     or dared to say to him, "You have done
     wrong"?*

(Job 36:22–23 JB)

*This was the answer Job gave to God:
I know that you are all-powerful:
     what you conceive, you can perform.
I am the man who obscured your designs
     with my empty-headed words.
I have been holding forth on matters I
     cannot understand,
     on marvels beyond me and my knowl-
     edge.*

(Job 42:1–3 JB)

Theologians have been battling for centuries over the question, How does a good, all-powerful God allow human suffering and evil? If he is all-good, then is he not all-powerful? If he is all-powerful, then is he not all-good? No matter your own theological bent—Calvinist or freewill—whether you say that God "causes" or "allows" suffering, the undeniable truth is that God is at the end of all the arguments and ultimately in control. Either God has his hand in its purpose or he does not interfere to stop it. He *is* all-powerful.

Three-year-old Kari is painfully dying of a brain tumor. Sandy, the teenage daughter of a leading Christian couple in their church, is brutally raped and murdered. Six-year-old Ryan is dying of AIDS resulting from a blood transfusion.

Some Christians say that God has his purpose in all human events. Others say that God never has a hand in evil, but then they must admit that God does not choose to stop the evil either. The arguments go round and round and are pointless when you are looking into the face of a parent whose child lies on a hospital bed and is covered by a sheet.

Effective helpers have not "figured it all out" nor do they have all the answers. Effective helpers put their arms around hurting people and say, "I don't understand either. But I love you and I'm here to go through it with you."

This is the model that the master helper, Jesus, gives us. He never promised us a life without suffering. He did promise his continuous love and presence:

For I am convinced that neither death nor life, neither angels nor demons, neither the present nor the future, nor any powers, neither height nor depth, nor anything else in all creation, will be able to separate us from the love of God that is in Christ Jesus our Lord (Rom. 8:38–39).

I have observed one distinct pattern in developing Christians. As they gain in maturity, they try to "figure God out" less, simply trust him, and put their effort into helping other people more. Trying to figure God out by analyzing the whys of his ways is very different from being solidly grounded in the scriptural truth of love and salvation that he gives us. These biblical Christians have learned how to "fly by the instruments."

Flying by the instruments is one of the most exciting concepts I learned in seminary. It compares a person living the Christian life to a pilot flying into the battle taking risks. The pilot can capably fly by his own sight when the weather is beautiful, but when the severe storms come, he has a choice. He can crash and be destroyed, or he can fly by the instruments—even when his instincts tell him to do otherwise—and survive. Flying by the instruments is trusting the truth of God's Word when the storms of life are upon us and we don't have time to figure it all out.

> *"Ships are safe in the harbor, but that is not what ships are for"*
>
> (anonymous)

Six scriptural truths to keep you steady and focused—instruments to fly by—during your battles follow.

Scriptural Truth 1: We are loved. We have salvation and eternal life.

> For God so loved the world that he gave his only begotten Son, that whosoever believeth in him should not perish, but have everlasting life (John 3:16 KJV).

The loss of a child, who brought us redemption, is the foundation of our Christian faith. God lost his Son, Jesus Christ, to death to save sinners. The reason for this tremendous sacrifice was that he loves us. God knows the parent's ache in watching a beloved child suffer and die. The comfort he offers us is solidly founded on empathy and compassion. Focusing on this fact has been the life preserver for many grieving Christian parents who have moved past anger and blaming God to surviving and effectively coping with their child's death. God never asks us to go through what he has not gone through himself. He goes before us to lead us and follows behind to protect and uphold us (Isa. 52:12).

Scriptural Truth 2: Our children are loved.

> Jesus said, "Let the little children come to me, and do not hinder them, for the kingdom of heaven belongs to such as these." When he had placed his hands on them, he went on from there (Matt. 19:14–15).

God loves not only us but our children as well. He holds them in his care. Little children are special to God just as they were special to our Lord Jesus. Jesus genuinely enjoyed the company of children. The disciples thought that they would be a nuisance to him, not worthy to take up his time. But Jesus stood firm; he wanted the children to come to him and even held them up to adults as the best examples of trusting followers. The children came, and Jesus held them, loved them, talked to them, and played with them. Perhaps children truly are closer than adults to the gates of heaven.

Scriptural Truth 3: We have his strength.

Cast your cares on the LORD,
    and he will sustain you;
    he will never let the righteous fall.
    (Ps. 55:22)

The most painful of all human experiences—losing a child to death—leaves families despaired, frail, weak, and without future hope for their days on earth. Getting out of bed to face one more day can be overwhelming. The pain never seems to numb even a little. We have no human resources for persevering in the face of this intense pain and devastation. But we do have God's resources. We have his unending strength. He can face the day when we can't face the next half-hour. He can carry us when we can't take the first step toward a life without our child. The beloved hymn of children everywhere tells us we are weak, but he is strong.

Jesus loves me, this I know,
For the Bible tells me so.
Little ones to him belong.
They are weak, but he is strong.

27

Scriptural Truth 4:
We have his comforting presence.

> Be strong, stand firm, have no fear of them, no terror, for
> Yahweh your God is going with you; he will not fail you
> or desert you (Deut. 31:6 JB).

There exists one fact in the Christian's life that cannot
be erased even in the most blinding of life's storms: God
has promised never to leave us. We may not feel his
presence in the consuming darkness, but he *is* there.
He is our Father, and we are his children. We can call
him "Daddy" just as Jesus did when he prayed "Abba
Father." His constant love, care, and presence never can
be taken from us, no matter how shattering life's circumstances may be.

Many grieving families have told me that in those
moments when the pain was unbearable they miraculously felt God's loving arms around them, holding them
tightly. It was an undeniable reality. He was there.

Scriptural Truth 5:
We have his protection from evil.

> We know that anyone born of God does not continue to
> sin; the one who was born of God keeps him safe, and
> the evil one cannot harm him. We know that we are
> children of God, and that the whole world is under the
> control of the evil one. We know also that the Son of
> God has come and has given us understanding, so that
> we may know him who is true. And we are in him who
> is true—even in his Son Jesus Christ. He is the true God
> and eternal life (1 John 5:18–20).

Pain touches us. Despair touches us. Suffering touches us. Death touches us. The whole range of human emotions and experiences touches us. But evil will *never* touch us. God promises to keep us safe and protect us from evil. We belong to God, and even in our weakest state he builds a fortress wall around us to keep the evil one out. God will fight evil for us. We can rest assured that we are safe.

Scriptural Truth 6: We can trust his purpose.

> Praise be to the God and Father of our Lord Jesus Christ, the Father of compassion and the God of all comfort, who comforts us in all our troubles, *so that we can comfort those in any trouble with the comfort we ourselves have received from God.* For just as the sufferings of Christ flow over into our lives, so also through Christ our comfort overflows. If we are distressed, it is for your comfort and salvation; if we are comforted, it is for your comfort, which produces in you patient endurance of the same sufferings we suffer. And our hope for you is firm, because we know that just as you share in our sufferings, so also you share in our comfort (2 Cor. 1:3–7, italics added).

We mere mortals do not like to suffer. We would never choose to suffer. But we cannot deny that suffering often brings great good and has ultimate purpose. Suffering of any kind—physical, spiritual, mental, or emotional—forces us to feel pain personally, to know it firsthand. No amount of intellectual input or professional training can substitute for personal experience. Those who have suffered greatly exhibit the most compassion, empathy, and desire to help others in similar situations. They are also the most effective helpers, because fellow sufferers know that their empathy is genuine and their expertise is proven.

God's purposes for us are to love others as he loves us and to mirror Jesus Christ. Grieving families who have reached out to love and support other grieving families hold the knowledge that their lives have great purpose.

Our Biblical Models:
Fellow Sufferers in Scripture

The Bible is as much a book about suffering and grieving as it is about love and salvation. Throughout Scripture we see that the children of God suffered and grieved over the loss of their loved ones. David, Job, Paul, Mary, and even Jesus were not exempt from the pain of loss; in fact, it was multiplied for them. Perhaps these fellow sufferers and the grievers of today have in common the higher calling.

Paul's Grief

> When he had said this, he knelt down with all of them and prayed. They all wept as they embraced him and kissed him. What grieved them most was his statement that they would never see his face again. Then they accompanied him to the ship. . . . After we had torn our-

selves away from them, we put out to sea and sailed straight to Cos (Acts 20:36–38; 21:1).

This treasure, tucked away in Acts, is a verse about relationship. It describes the essence of our Christian faith. God loves us deeply. He calls us out to love him deeply and to love others as an extension of that love. Because we love deeply, the pain will be intense when the relationship is severed. At some point every human relationship on this earth is severed. Death is the surest fact of our human existence.

The people at Ephesus were not losing Paul to death, but they felt the same intensity of pain, for they knew that they would not see him again in this life. The separation would be permanent. Paul had to tear himself away from his dear friends; the hurt of being torn apart was very real. There is nothing clean and easy in severing intimate relationships; it does feel like being ripped in two. Because God's people love deeply, they grieve deeply—in Paul's day as well as in ours. Later when Paul faced his own death, he asked Timothy to "come before winter" so that they could be together one last time to say good-bye. Paul was a man committed to relationships. He is our fellow griever.

David's Grief

David knew grief well. Could we have survived the following?

David mourned the loss of his dearest friend, Jonathan.

He lost the first son whom he and Bathsheba had conceived to grave illness. He understood this tragedy as a judgment on his sin. He had fasted and pleaded with God to spare his son and then accepted the finality of his death.

On returning to Ziklag to discover that the town had been burned and their families taken captive by the Amalekites, David and his men had "wept aloud till they were too weak to weep anymore" (1 Sam. 30:4).

David was to suffer one more grief, which was less bearable than any of the preceding ones—the brutal murder of his beloved son Absalom.

> The king shuddered. He went up to the room over the gate and burst into tears, and weeping said, "My son Absalom! My son! My son Absalom! Would I had died in your place! Absalom, my son, my son!" Word was brought to Joab, "The king is now weeping and mourning for Absalom." And the day's victory was turned to mourning for all the troops, because they learned that the king was grieving for his son. And the troops returned stealthily that day to the town, as troops creep back ashamed when routed in battle. The king had veiled his face and was crying aloud, "My son Absalom! Absalom, my son, my son" (2 Sam. 19:1–4 JB).

David is our fellow griever.

Job's Grief

Job lost everything—his entire estate, the support of his wife and friends, his health—but his most painful loss was of his ten children in one accident, where severe wind crushed the house around them. God allowed Job to be severely tested by Satan. Job was a man in deep depression and despair. He wanted to die, but he did not sin. He did not turn away from God.

> "If we take happiness from God's hand, must we not take sorrow too?" And in all this misfortune Job uttered no sinful word (Job 2:10 JB).

Job is our fellow griever.

Mary's Grief

> Near the cross of Jesus stood his mother, his mother's sister, Mary the wife of Clopas, and Mary Magdalene. When Jesus saw his mother there, and the disciple whom he loved standing nearby, he said to his mother, "Dear woman, here is your son," and to the disciple, "Here is your mother." From that time on, this disciple took her into his home (John 19:25–27).

Can you imagine helplessly watching your child be tortured, mocked, and executed before your eyes? Mary watched the slaughter of her precious gift from God, knowing that her son had done nothing wrong. Her grief and rage must have been almost uncontrollable. Notice that Mary's sister and Mary of Magdala were by her side to comfort her through his hideous ordeal.

Jesus, God himself, knew her pain and asked his disciple to care for her, thereby creating a new family. Imagine how Mary and her "new son" must have supported one another through their grief. God does not intend for us to grieve alone—not during the ordeal of a loved one's death nor afterward.

Jesus' Grief

Jesus wept.
Then the Jews said, "See how he loved him!"
But some of them said, "Could not he who opened the eyes of the blind man have kept this man from dying?" (John 11:35–37).

We of finite human mind do not comprehend why Jesus would weep and grieve for Lazarus when he knew that he was about to raise him from the dead. Perhaps this is our greatest lesson in grief counseling. Jesus was moved by the pain of Lazarus's sisters and friends and immediately entered into their grief. He cried with them and felt their pain *first*, then went to raise Lazarus from the dead. Jesus put their relationship ahead of his power to solve their problem.

Jesus understood human grief, evidenced by the lengths he went to prepare his dearest friends, the disciples, for his death. He knew that the more the disciples understood about his coming death and were prepared for it, the better they could cope. Jesus needed to say good-bye and prepare for his own death. He told his friends that this would be a time for grief.

I tell you the truth, you will weep and mourn while the world rejoices. You will grieve, but your grief will turn to joy. A woman giving birth to a child has pain because her time has come; but when her baby is born she forgets the anguish because of her joy that a child is born into the world. So with you: Now is your time of grief, but I will see you again and you will rejoice, and no one will take away your joy (John 16:20–22).

35

This is the relevant message for all of us. Now is a time of grief and earthly separation, but then we will know great joy in eternity. Jesus understands our grief.

Violent Death

Losing a loved one to violent death is the most painful of human griefs, and the early Christians were no strangers to that pain.

> Some were tortured, refusing to accept release, that they might rise again to a better life. Others suffered mocking and scourging, and even chains and imprisonment. They were stoned, they were sawn in two, they were killed with the sword; they went about in skins of sheep and goats, destitute, afflicted, ill-treated—of whom the world was not worthy—wandering over deserts and mountains, and in dens and caves of the earth. And all these, though well attested by their faith, did not receive what was promised, since God had foreseen something better for us, that apart from us they should not be made perfect (Heb. 11:35–40 RSV).

What does this passage say? Does God break his promises to his faithful children? No! And here lies the key to understanding suffering. Note the preceding verses to this passage:

> And what more shall I say? For time would fail me to tell of Gideon, Barak, Samson, Jephthah, of David and Samuel and the prophets—who through faith conquered kingdoms, enforced justice, received promises, stopped the mouths of lions, quenched raging fire, escaped the edge of the sword, won strength out of weakness, became mighty in war, put foreign armies to flight.

Women received their dead by resurrection (Heb. 11:32–35 RSV).

These faithful men did receive God's promises. These victorious men (vv. 32–35) as well as the sufferers (vv. 35–39) and their grieving families who must have watched them die, had the *same faith* in God—the same salvation that you and I have. Yet their earthly outcomes were different.

The faith described in Hebrews 11:32–35 has been called "Noah faith." These men were spared from suffering; God delivered them *from* tribulation.

The faith described in Hebrews 11:35–39 has been called "Job faith." These men who were called to die for their faith were delivered *through* suffering, just as Job suffered for his unshakable faith in God.[1]

God's promises stand firm. His faithful children are saved and delivered—sometimes *from* suffering and sometimes *through* suffering.

Grievers search for fellow journeyers to share their sorrow. The Scriptures offer an invaluable source of godly men and women, including our own precious Lord, who have known their pain.

Fellow Grief Counselor: Isaiah

Isaiah is God's biblical model for a grief counselor. We know Isaiah as prophet, but his role as pastoral grief counselor is less well known. In Isaiah's time, a counselor was defined as "one who knew God's plan." Counseling was an extension of prophecy.

Hezekiah lay ill and dying. Isaiah immediately communicated God's will to him: "Yahweh says this, 'Put your affairs in order, for you are going to die, you will not live'" (Isaiah 38:2 JB).

God is honest with Hezekiah through the prophet. He does not hide the fact of the king's coming death; instead he offers Hezekiah the opportunity to prepare for it. Grief counselors of our century have only recently discovered this important practice.

Hezekiah's response is to pray to God: "Ah, Yahweh, remember, I beg you, how I have behaved faithfully and with sincerity of heart in your presence and done what is right in your eyes" (Isa. 38:3 JB).

Hezekiah does not ask God to change the circumstances. He simply asks to be remembered for his loyalty and focuses on his relationship with God. Then Hezekiah weeps. The king feels his grief deeply and does not hesitate to show his emotions.

God hears his prayers and sees his tears (38:5) and adds fifteen years to Hezekiah's life. God clearly controls the length of our lives as he chooses. God entered into Hezekiah's circumstances and felt his emotions. As helpers, we must communicate the fact that God feels the griever's pain. Being in control, God intervened to change Hezekiah's situation. Isaiah asks for a fig poultice to be brought and applied to Hezekiah's ulcer as medicine. God does use his creation in accomplishing his purposes.

Hezekiah's Canticle

Following his recovery, Hezekiah composed a canticle (the combination of poetry and song) to express his journey of suffering. Note the stages of grief that he walked through.

38:10	Anger and desperation	Hezekiah faces the frustration of dying before his time on earth should be finished ("in the noon of life"). He experiences angry despair.
38:11–13	Helplessness	Hezekiah imagines the actual experience of death ("like a weaver, you roll up my life and cut it from the loom.") He experiences helplessness.
38:14–15	Reconciliation with God	Hezekiah communicates with God, asking for protection. He understands that God is in control by causing his illness or removing it.
38:18–20	Deeper understanding of God's purposes	Hezekiah has a deeper understanding of death and life through God. He desires to share God's mercy with others ("Fathers tell their children about your faithfulness").

Is it possible that his "therapist," Isaiah, directed Hezekiah to compose the canticle to release his pain?

The key to Isaiah's effective counseling of Hezekiah was that they had a prior relationship rooted in God's principles. Isaiah's God-given role was to communicate the nature and will of God, and God consistently advised Hezekiah for many years. Isaiah was available to the king throughout his reign, in good times and bad. He stood by to support Hezekiah when the king ignored his advice and disobeyed God. Isaiah was committed to that cause. Hezekiah was a good king and worked for reform. His downfall lay in his sometimes thinking that his plans (e.g., the siege of 701 B.C.) were an improvement on God's ways. Isaiah cultivated a consistent, unconditional, loving friendship with Hezekiah and was a mirror of God's love. Because he had earned Hezekiah's trust, Isaiah was able to counsel him effectively when he lay dying. He was honest with the king about his coming death and helped him prepare for it, while at the same time he offered God's message of hope. We helpers of today are called to do the same.

5

When Suffering Turns to Gold

Severe suffering breeds two responses in human beings: bitterness and anger, or love and compassion. It never breeds indifference. Sufferers turn to God or away from God. The key result is that whatever is the final response toward God will be the suffering person's response toward others. Sufferers who have survived crises either hate more or love more. I tell you two very different stories: one about a hater and one about a lover.

Mary often had arguments with her only son, Tom. He was as strong an individual as she was, and both had explosive tempers. At one family dinner at Tom's house, Mary vehemently opposed the way Tom was disciplining his children. She finally stormed out of the house and refused to speak to Tom for weeks. Then,

Tom's family left on a vacation where Tom died in a tragic accident.

Mary was left broken. She not only had to grieve the loss of her only son but also the loss of any opportunity to reconcile their relationship. Her brokenness turned to hatred—hatred toward God, family, and friends. Her grief poisoned her.

Victoria and Mike, a dedicated Christian couple, were on vacation camping in the mountains with their family when their two-and-a-half-year-old daughter began to have severe respiratory problems. They rushed her to the hospital for tests, and a few days later they learned that she had the terminal illness cystic fibrosis.

Victoria and Mike were devastated. They experienced the struggles common to parents facing a child's death. They were despaired, had marital struggles because of the intense pressure on their relationship, dealt with severe depression and thoughts of suicide, and suffered exhaustion because of the new routines of medical care required for their daughter. They also had to continue to care for their infant son.

Victoria told me that the most painful times came as she stroked her daughter's hair while she slept in the middle of the night and knew the child would die and her bed would be empty soon. The pain seemed unbearable. Victoria realized that she faced a decision. She could shake her fist in anger at God or she could praise and trust his purpose in this suffering.

Victoria and Mike chose to thank and trust God. They joined a support group for parents of dying children and reached out to the other members. They shared their testimony of peace with their daughter's doctors, nurses, and other hospital staff. Victoria was able to lead a non-Christian friend who was dying of cancer on a journey to faith in Jesus Christ. This friend would not share her struggles with death or anger toward God with anyone else. Victoria was the only one who understood, because she walked the same road with her daughter.

Victoria and Mike used their tragedy to reach out and minister to anyone God brought in their path. Their compassion and love increased daily. Their lives had purpose; their suffering had turned to gold.[1]

> Is any one of you sick? He should call the elders of the church to pray over him and anoint him with oil in the name of the Lord. And the prayer offered in faith will make the sick person well; the Lord will raise him up. If he has sinned, he will be forgiven (James 5:14–15).

Sixteen-year-old Linda was dying of cancer. She and her family were strong evangelical Christians. Her pastor came to visit often. I was able to include spiritual songs in our music therapy sessions and discuss our common faith. Linda thought that her illness was the result of a sin she had committed recently and that since she had repented she would be healed. Her parents were unaware of that "particular sin" or that Linda felt responsible. She never told them. They, too, had faith that she would be healed.

The deacons of their church came to pray and put oil on Linda. But she was not healed and died soon after. The night of her death, Linda's family, friends, and deacons of their church surrounded her still body on the hospital bed. They lit candles in the hospital room. They believed that God could and would still heal her; they prayed that she would be raised from the dead. However, Linda had already gone home. Their faith was shattered and their grief unbearable.

Victoria and Mike's story had a different outcome. Shortly after Amanda's diagnosis, the deacons came to pray and anoint her with oil. Four years after Amanda's diagnosis and months of suffering, she was healed. To this day she never has had another symptom. On receiving news of her clean health, most of Amanda's doctors on her treatment team said that she must have been misdiagnosed initially. They could not account for the complete disappearance of her symptoms. The one Christian doctor on the team said, "Yes, she was healed."

A very sad but common phenomenon occurred to Victoria and Mike following Amanda's healing: They lost their opportunity to minister to other families with terminally ill children. There was no reason for Victoria and Mike to continue to attend the support group meetings. Just their presence was a painful reminder to the other families that their children were not healed.

Victoria and Mike's best friends in the group, another Christian couple who had taken Victoria and Mike under their wing, lost their daughter to death the same month that Amanda was healed. It is a simple truth that human beings accept ministry more readily from fellow sufferers than from those who do not share their pain. This opportunity to care for other hurting people is the golden thread in the purpose of suffering.

Amanda was healed; Linda was not healed. For every Amanda there are thousands of Lindas. God can and does heal people, but it is not the more frequent occurrence. Healing is the mystery of his ways. There is no magic formula to procure it, no "particular action of faith" in which the healed one engaged that the unhealed did not. God in his sovereignty knows best.

While working at the hospital I began to observe that often the patients most precious to me, with parents of the most sincere faith, were the unhealed. It occurred to me that perhaps there are two kinds of healing, two kinds of gold: temporary healing for life on this earth, and ultimate healing for life with God. When these families prayed for healing, perhaps God gave their children "ultimate healing" for eternity with him. Parents prayed for happy, pain-free, well lives for their children, and God bestowed it on them—never to be taken away again. It was not that God didn't answer their prayers or say no; perhaps his answer was a permanent yes.

A view of ultimate healing does not diminish the pain of the grievers, though. Therefore, the helper's response of shared struggle must be the same: to support the family, never to analyze the circumstances. God's ways may be a mystery, but our job is not. The Scriptures clearly direct us to "rejoice with those who rejoice and mourn with those who mourn."

PART 2

Taking the Journey: Helping the Dying Child

To *want* to help is different from knowing *how* to help. To effectively help hurting people requires specialized skills and knowledge. We will see that skills for helping the dying child are different from skills for helping the grieving family.

Helping Through the Illness and Hospitalization

Our first priority as helpers is to help the *child*. Pastoral care to sick children is too often a neglected field in Christian ministry. Pastors and chaplains are comfortable offering pastoral care to adults. Youth workers are comfortable educating and discipling young people. But no specialization exists that provides pastoral care to hurting children.

When a child is dying, most pastors and chaplains traditionally support the family. They know how to offer comfort to the adult parents, which is definitely needed, but this is the vicious circle: Whereas it is true that support for parents will enable them to comfort their child, in reality, *the most effective way to help the parents is to directly help the child.*

Finding the Right Hospital

Dying children must deal with medical procedures and hospitalization. Hospitalization ranks as one of the most stressful events that a child can experience. If not handled properly, it can be a most frightening and traumatic crisis. Your first task is to help the child and family cope with hospitalization. For most dying children, the hospital will become the world in which they live.

To begin, it is important to understand the difference between a children's hospital and a pediatric wing of a general hospital. A children's hospital focuses entirely on children. Most general hospitals cannot afford to do this. A children's hospital will have a child-life program and philosophy that commits it to the total well-being of the child and family. The staff will do what is best for the child, not what is more convenient for them. (Any parent knows that what children need usually is not convenient for adults.) Whether you help the parents investigate a children's hospital or that exceptional pediatric wing of a general hospital, check to see if it has the following offerings.

Is there a preadmission tour?

Many pediatric programs offer a weekly hospital tour for incoming patients and their families. The children can view the different areas of the hospital and then *go home* to think about it. Some group programs have a small party after the tour, complete with refreshments, a movie about "going to the hospital," and hospital souvenirs to take home. This event helps the child to actually look forward to returning to the hospital. Often terminally ill patients will be hospitalized immediately after diagnosis, with no option to attend a tour. Yet, ideally patients would have the chance to be introduced to the hospital first.

Are there visiting hours? May siblings visit?

Children do not operate on adult clocks. Pediatric hospitals do not have visiting hours. Parents, siblings, and friends can come whenever it is convenient for the child. Some innovative hospitals even allow pets to visit.

Can parents remain with the child for the entire stay?
Can parents sleep in the room at night?

The most serious part of a hospital stay for any child is the fear of being alone and separated from loved ones and familiar surroundings. Separation anxiety can be far more serious than a medical problem. Advise parents not to choose a hospital where they are not permitted to stay an entire day or spend the night with their child.

Will parents be able to give input about their child and be part of the health-care team?

The parents know their child better than anyone, and most doctors and nurses respect this. The staff should welcome parents' insights about their child and inform them about medical procedures at every stage of the illness. Caring doctors and nurses who take the time to talk with families are crucial.

Is there a child-life program? Is there a playroom?

The child-life program of a pediatric program is staffed by professional educators and therapists. Their sole purpose is to insure the total well-being of the patient—emotionally, mentally, and physically. There should be a central playroom where group, as well as individual, activities are offered. The playroom is the "safe retreat" in the hospital. No painful procedures are allowed there. When children cannot visit the playroom, a therapist can work with them in their rooms.

The playroom is the natural setting to develop relationships. Patients make friends with other patients, parents meet each other, and a common support base is built.

Teen retreat lounges can be found in adolescent units. Infant stimulation programs are available for babies. Be aware of appropriate programs for the patient's age.

Child-Life Therapy Techniques with Hospitalized Children

The hospital experience that is handled correctly can contribute positively to a child's development, whereas a negative experience can cause anxiety, fear, withdrawal, regression, defiance, and delay the physical healing process. The child-life program provides "total person care" for each patient as well as for the family. It exists to minimize the trauma of hospitalization and is concerned with meeting the emotional and developmental needs of patients. The child-life approach is not a frill. It is a known fact in pediatric health care that happy and busy children get well faster.

Professional educators and therapists who work in the child-life department are termed child-life specialists and are certified by a national council. They plan therapeutic activities and interact with the pediatric health team composed of doctors, nurses, social workers, psychologists, dieticians, therapists, and chaplains. This team is committed to the physical and emotional well-being of the patient.

A myriad of backgrounds create an effective child-life staff. Some child-life specialists are certified teachers who continue the patient's educational program in the hospital during the absence from school. Some are recreational therapists. Others are child development specialists or have pediatric nursing backgrounds to deal with medical issues. Since creative expression is an established effective way to cope with the stress of hospitalization and illness, others are creative-arts therapists. Child-life specialists integrate a number of therapy methods to best help their patients. You the helper can learn from them, do the same, and also teach parents how to help their children.

An overview of therapy techniques follows.

Medical Play Therapy and Preparation

Play therapy is the primary tool employed by child-life specialists to help children cope with the stress of hospitalization. Play is the children's work; it is their medium of self-expression and the way they master anxiety. Through play, children gain control over real-life situations in which they feel helpless.

Play is the one activity which provides continuity between the hospital and the normalcy of the outside world and also serves as a diagnostic tool to observe the patient's reactions to hospitalization. Medical play therapy is a specialized area of play therapy.

The unknown is frightening. Hospitalized children should be told what will happen to them. From the smallest medical test (such as a blood test) to major surgery, every procedure should be fully explained to the child beforehand. This is *medical preparation*, achieved through education. Puppets, videotapes, and children's hospital books are examples of teaching tools to inform children. Medical play therapy offers patients the opportunity to have control as "doctor" and play out hospital procedures on dolls, stuffed animals, parents, or therapists with realistic medical equipment in a safe environment. The patient engages in medical play therapy before having an actual medical procedure to gain an understanding of what will take place; it gives the helper the opportunity to clear up any misconceptions. It is just as important for the patient to engage in medical play therapy after the procedure to work through any trauma and cope with the experience. This clues the therapist as to what the patient is feeling.

Bibliotherapy is the use of books in therapy. Children's books on hospitals and medical procedures are used to educate and prepare the patient as well as provide an opportunity to discuss the child's questions, fears, and concerns. It is the relationship of the helper reading to the child that is key, not the book itself. The book is the tool. Bibliotherapy extends to reading books which bring up different emotions that the child can relate to and discuss—books about other hurting children, or fantasies which distract patients from pain and help them leave the world of the hospital for a while. Christian helpers will want to use books about scriptural truth and God's love and care.

Verbalization

The primary goal common to all therapy methods is to help children verbalize their feelings and discuss their fears and concerns about hospital experiences in a loving and accepting environment. Pediatric experts agree that a child needs to talk about the hospital experience to be able to cope with it. Verbalization *precedes* understanding and mastery of anxiety.

To want to listen to children open up about their concerns is not enough. Children are people of action; they are *doers*. They will talk to someone when they are involved in an activity—doing something—with that person. Traditional counseling approaches often result in the child's silence. Whether you the helper are playing a game, reading a book, "doctoring" a doll, or singing songs with the child, your task is to provide a safe environment where you can establish a relationship of trust with the patient and he or she can *talk to you*. Recreational activities provide that framework.

Creative-Arts Therapies

Creative expression through artistic experience is an established method for coping with the trauma of hospitalization. The creative-arts therapies are ideal for the hospitalized child because they offer: (1) an element of play; (2) an opportunity for creative expression and release; and (3) a safe environment for sharing concerns. Since the artistic medium is comforting, non-threatening, and not associated with medical procedures, the therapist can quickly establish a relationship of trust with the patient.

The creative arts therapies include art, music, dance, and drama/puppet therapy, with creative writing as an extension of these fields. Though the medium is different, the principles are the same in each process. The therapist employs his or her artistic medium as the tool in treating the patient's problem area.

Let us define music therapy as a specific example. Music making is an effective tool because it is one of the few processes that involve all our modalities—visual, auditory, motor, emotional, cognitive, etc. It is cross-modal. While music therapy employs a strong developmental area which is comfortable for the child, a weak developmental area can simultaneously be treated. The child is distracted from his limitations and the disorder is more easily treated.

Music therapy in the clinical setting can help an accident victim to regain the use of his hands through his learning to play an instrument. It relieves pain and stress through imagery and relaxation techniques. Music therapy uses familiar songs to prompt terminally ill patients to discuss life experiences and prepare for death. It teaches children how to socialize through musical games, or helps a newborn infant discover his environment. Music therapy teaches individuals with respiratory or speech problems to sing. It implements group music activities to enhance self-esteem. Music therapy employs musical games and songs to encourage a child abuse victim to discuss her experience or to distract a pediatric patient from the pain and trauma of hospitalization. The applications are endless. The need is identified first, and the musical experience is tailored to meet it.

In the hospital, music activities are a form of play for pediatric patients, offering normal avenues for growth and development and providing continuity between the hospital and the child's outside world. The medium of music meets the patient's need for creative expression and channeling of anxiety. Music therapy group activities conducted in the child-life playroom allow patients to share with one another and offer mutual support. Yet the most effective use of music therapy is providing the framework for verbalization. Original compositions, creating new lyrics for familiar songs, or fill-in-the-blank songs are opportunities for discussion of feelings.

Artistic processes are also diagnostic tools. Helpers learn what a patient feels and perceives through his or her creative expression. Like original music, artwork is an excellent clue to what children understand about their hospitalization. Drawing self-pictures shows how children view what is happening to their bodies.

In my work I guided patients in creating a large weaving. We worked on it together much as in an old-fashioned quilting bee. Each patient created one section and enjoyed explaining how his or her color choices reflected hospital life. Proud patients helped hang it on a hospital wall for all to see.

Creative dramatics and puppetry are another powerful medium for children to communicate their fears. It is much easier to talk to a dog puppet named Floppy than a strange hospital worker. Movement therapists help patients adapt to their loss of mobility. Children become frustrated when they cannot move. Therapists focus on what patients can do, not what they cannot do. Maybe a bedridden patient can only move one arm; she can create "arm dances" and imagine moving her entire body.[1]

By writing poetry, painting pictures, creating group murals, composing music about hospitalization, or enacting their experiences through drama and movement, patients share their concerns with others and cope with the crisis of illness.

The most exciting aspect of the creative-arts therapies is that their use is biblically based. What did David do when he struggled? He expressed his suffering through writing psalms. It is a rare reference in Scripture where praise of God and communication through prayer is not linked with music making. Song was a weapon in the spiritual life. Jesus understood the power of music in facing trial. The last event he and his disciples shared before departing the upper room for the Mount of Olives was to sing psalms together (Matt. 26:30). Paul and Silas sang hymns of praise with their feet in stocks in prison (Acts 16:25). Note that David may have been the first known music therapist:

Now the Spirit of the Lord departed from Saul, and an evil spirit from the Lord tormented him. And Saul's servants said to him, "Behold now, an evil spirit from God is tormenting you. Let our lord now command your servants, who are before you, to seek out a man who is skilful in playing the lyre; and when the evil spirit from God is upon you, he will play it, and you will be well." . . . And whenever the evil spirit from God was upon Saul, David took the lyre and played it with his hand; so Saul was refreshed, and was well, and the evil spirit departed from him (1 Sam. 16:14–17, 23 RSV).

Music is inseparable from God's presence.

Respect for the Child

Respecting the patient and being his or her advocate is another important part of the helper's job. You must continually affirm that the child can trust you. In addition to helping patients cope with hospitalization through use of the above therapy techniques, you should also keep in mind the following:

1. Make sure that the patient is as comfortable and enjoying as normal an environment as possible. Encourage children to bring their favorite possessions from home. Help patients with continued schoolwork. Keep disruption of the normal lifestyle to a minimum.
2. Never surprise a child. No one should be allowed to perform a procedure on a child without fully explaining it first.
3. Always tell the truth. The rule is that if a procedure is going to hurt, tell the child it will hurt.

4. Do not "talk around" the child. Discourage others from talking about the child's medical problems as if the child were not present. Include the patient in the conversation.
5. Give the patient some control. For example, one cannot give the child the choice of whether or not he wants a shot, but one can ask him which arm he chooses to have it in. Children become frightened when they feel helpless in their situation.

Pastoral Care

Pastoral care to hospitalized children ideally is the integration of God's truth with effective therapy methods. It begins with the helper—the therapist/minister who reflects Jesus Christ and builds a relationship with the child that mirrors God's constant love and care. The child should "see Jesus" in you, the helper.

Your love and concern for the child overflow to his or her family. You care for them through helping their child and being available to support them through the trauma of hospitalization and the coming death. The key is an established relationship and bond of trust and love.

Each therapy process discussed above can be applied in a spiritual context. While acting out medical play therapy, you can discuss how God is in control, made our bodies, and will guide the doctors in procedures. You can assure patients that God never leaves them, even in the hospital. While everyone is unsure of the future, Christians can trust God to have carefully planned every step.

Bibliotherapy can include books about God's care for us and other biblical truths. The Bible, God's guidebook for life, is certainly the ultimate tool in bibliotherapy.

You can share Scripture passages that are presented to helpers in part 1 of this book. You can help patients verbalize their feelings to you and to God through prayer, creative writing, composing songs, and singing hymns.

You are probably discovering that effective therapy methods are simply God's biblical methods for helping his children deal with pain "in secular language." When you help within a secular institution or support nonbelievers, you are still an ambassador of Jesus Christ. You communicate God's biblical truths of love and comfort in action. Even the most confirmed atheist when faced with his dying child will shake a fist angrily at God and say, "How could God do this to me?" It, too, is communication with God and an opportunity for ministry.

You can minister to hospitalized children by providing effective ways to cope that are rooted in God's love and care. Tangible skills for helping go hand-in-hand with your spiritual commitment.

In summary, then, your primary tasks are to directly help the child in these ways:

1. Support the family as they hospitalize their child. Be their advocate.
2. Educate parents about hospitals and the rights of pediatric patients.
3. Apply therapy techniques to help the child cope with the trauma of hospitalization. You should be

familiar with play therapy, medical play therapy, creative-arts therapies, pastoral care principles, and the use of Scripture.

4. Remember that helping children to verbalize their experiences is your goal. If you are uncomfortable with music and arts activities or play therapy/counseling techniques, you may enjoy playing board games, reading books, using puppets, or playing doctor.

5. The key is to help children talk to you. Listen carefully to learn their struggles and fears. Creative-arts expression is especially important with patients who have trouble verbalizing.

6. Most important, you are the mirror of Jesus Christ. Assure children of God's love and faithfulness. Help them communicate with God through informal prayer, Scripture, music, and creative writing.

7. Surrounding dying children with relationships of love and trust (with God, their families, and you the helper) is the foundation of their journey home.

7

Helping Patients and Families Through the Death

We now move from helping the child and family cope with hospitalization to preparing them for the death. The child will die in a hospital, hospice (health-care facility for treatment of the terminally ill), or at home. *Hospice* means a team approach of total-person care to meet all needs of the patient and family and may or may not include a separate location to die. It is an extension of child-life care for the pediatric patient. Since most hospices do not have a child-life specialization, the majority of pediatric patients die in a children's hospital. Others die at home. Home care of the dying, where the health-care team works with the family to treat patients in their home environment, is an option. Helpers bring the same skills to hospital, hospice, or home.

Who can best help the child die is the child's *own family*. Your task is to help them do that. It is no surprise that the family begins the grieving process when they first learn of the terminal illness. Often they become so lost in their own grief they fail to realize that they have an important job to do—to help their child die. That is hard work, which requires full involvement, and is radically different from the natural human tendency to distance oneself from a patient in the final stages of illness to avoid further pain. The helper must realize that he or she can fall into this trap, too.

If the parents begin pulling away before the death and do not grab on to the final opportunities to spend time with their child, their preparation will be less and their grief work will be that much harder after the death. The family must enter with the child into the *reality* of the dying process.

Help families to build final memories—to take that last vacation trip, to fully celebrate that last Christmas or their child's last birthday. They celebrate these special, bittersweet days in a way we can never understand. Families know they must live these times to their fullest. Free them from any responsibilities that will stand in their way.

Siblings must be part of the process and not be shut out "for their own good." That will only intensify their pain and confuse them. The amount of involvement will, of course, depend on the ages of the siblings. The death should be talked about openly and honestly. Nothing should be hidden. There should be room for plenty of questions and no atmosphere of secrecy in the home.

Siblings should be included, not excluded, from activities such as visiting the child in the hospital. The dying process needs to be a family matter that includes grandparents and other extended-family members.

How much the patient or siblings understand about the coming death depends on their developmental concept of death as well as their faith in Jesus Christ. The preschooler who thinks that her brother will come back is not "denying death"; this is simply how young children view death—as a temporary and reversible happening. This is the age of active imagination, where fact and fantasy are interchanged. The preschooler's grief is intense with a wide range of emotion, brief, and requires repeated explanations of the death. (This is especially painful for parents.) Rituals are helpful.

Preschoolers can view death as a punishment for breaking rules or as a result of their wishing it. A young child who "wished his brother would die" when he was angry with him can actually think that he caused his death. You can assure preschoolers that God loves them unconditionally and would never punish them. Small children think that their deceased siblings will go on living in different circumstances. You can affirm that a brother or sister who trusted Jesus Christ now lives in heaven with him.

Preschoolers live in the present, not the future. The dying preschool patient will be more concerned about today's trauma of pain, what is happening to his or her body, and the family's reactions to the illness than the lost tomorrow. True grief comes from understanding that death is a lost future, but this loss is not a reality for the young child. You can promise preschoolers that you will help thcm live today and that God holds their futures in his hands.

By age seven the child is aware that dying means losing loved ones, and this realization of separation can cause fear. The middle-age child sees death as a person coming to take someone away. Depending on individual maturity, the child may still have some early preschool concepts of death, but he begins to understand that death is permanent and can conceive of an afterlife. You can assure these children that God only wants the best for them and is not a villain coming to take their loved one away.

Adolescents deal with death by employing adult coping mechanisms (such as, denial, repression, and anger); they finally move into acceptance. They understand death is final. The teenage years can be the most difficult during which to face one's own death. Two major focuses of this age are on physical appearance and social standing and on setting goals and making future plans (living in the future). Death robs teens of both. Teenagers are often as traumatized by the way they look because of their illness, especially from radiation treatments for cancer, and distance from their friends as they are by their coming death. They lose the purpose for having dreams, planning, and achieving future goals. Grieving adolescent siblings will also need to enter adult grief work (as discussed in chapter 9).

Facing death in God's truth does make all the difference. It is the difference between death and life—an eternal life in Jesus Christ. Christian helpers can offer a facet of care to the dying and their families that secular helpers cannot. You can offer hope and eternal healing. When dying children fear separation from their families, you can promise that their big daddy, God, and their best friend, Jesus, will never leave them. When they fear an end to life, God promises them a better, unending life. When a grieving sibling says that her sister is alive somewhere else, you can say that she is right. When adolescents hate how they look, you can verify that they are beautiful to God and that he is planning heavenly goals for them. When patients fear the disease process in their bodies, you can tell them that God made their bodies, knows what he is doing, and will guide the doctor.

The same methods for helping the child cope with hospitalization remain the most effective methods for coping with death. Death must be an open topic to be dealt with. The coming death should never be hidden from the child.

Children cannot be fooled. They sense when talk about death makes adults uncomfortable. Children who were outgoing and expressive will become withdrawn and appear to experience a personality change when they face death. In reality, they have simply learned that their families cannot talk about the death nor hear their concerns, so they keep them to themselves.

Preparation for medical procedures and education about what is happening to the patient's body in the disease process should be continued, with opportunity for play therapy. The use of books and the creative-arts therapies will help the patient verbalize and express his feelings and concerns about death. Music is an excellent tool for providing safety and comfort in the final stages of death. Hearing is the last sense to leave the dying body.

The actual activities obviously need to be tailored for the child's individual age. Medical preparation, books, and creative-arts activities will be different for the three-year-old than the fifteen-year-old. This requires the helper to have researched a variety of resources for different ages and know the individual likes and dislikes of each child.

No matter the method, your first goal is to provide an accepting atmosphere where the patient can talk about and understand death and help the family to do the same. Be familiar with local organizations, support groups, and literature which you can recommend. (See part 4 of this book for a listing of resources.)

A second goal is to create as normal an environment as possible with short-term goals and projects. This is why dying young children learn to read, older children do their homework up to the week of their death, and parents still discipline disobedient behavior. This helps patients have hope and purpose for today. The worst thing is to encourage them to give up living the life that they do have left.

Your role as helper is twofold: (1) to fully enter the grief process and share the patient's and family's present pain; and (2) offer them a foundation and future hope in Jesus Christ. This integration of God's message with our human lives of suffering is the essence of the gospel.

To summarize, remember to do the following:

1. Help the family help their child die. Help parents and siblings to be wholly involved in their child's dying process. Encourage open, honest communication, with no secrets.
2. Be aware of the children's concepts of death that correspond to their age. Help siblings to grieve at their levels of maturity. Discuss topics which may be too painful for the parents.
3. Discuss death as a coming reality. Help dying children grieve their own deaths. Affirm God's constant love and care and eternal life in Jesus Christ.
4. Maintain a normal environment with short-term goals for the dying child.
5. Be familiar with resource organizations, support groups, and literature to advise the family.
6. Prepare yourself to grieve.

Zain's Journey:
Advice from the Experts

This chapter is an account of the journey of a young man who knew how to die and the parents who knew how to help him.[1]

In his family's eyes, December 4, 1985, is Zain's "birthday." It is the day that twelve-year-old Zain died of a brain tumor and was born into the Kingdom of God. One week before Zain's death, a family friend died of a heart attack. Zain's family was comforted because they believed that this dear friend had gone before to wait for Zain. Zain was not without plenty of friends on earth; he would not be without friends in heaven. He loved God as his parents did. He was bright, friendly, loving, and enjoyed life to the fullest.

During the summer of 1984, Zain's family was making a trip up the California coast when Zain began to have recurring stomach sickness. A few weeks later, he began to have terrible headaches. The first doctor who saw Zain said that Zain's problem was psychosomatic. Zain's parents, Kathy and David, persevered, and a series of doctors and tests revealed that Zain had a rapidly growing brain tumor. There was little hope for his survival. It would be a matter of months before his death.

The doctors were honest; chemotherapy and radiation could prolong his life a little, but the treatments would cause Zain great misery and never cure him. Zain's parents decided not to pursue those treatments. They opted for alternative medicines that had no side effects. Kathy and David prayed for Zain's healing. They also prayed that if God still chose to take him, Zain would be as healthy as possible for their last few months together.

God did not heal Zain on earth, but he did protect him from great pain and suffering and allow him to lead a relatively normal, healthy life. Zain graduated with honors from sixth grade in June. He was an excellent student and up until the night before he died was concerned about finishing his homework. Kathy and David felt that God was very tender with them. Their last months together were wonderful and provided them with memories that would last a lifetime. Zain continued to love and trust his Lord, and he and his family thanked God for every "one more day" that they were allowed to spend together. Zain and his family believed strongly in the purpose of his illness and the special job that Zain had been given. And then one Sunday morning in December Zain got up in church and gave hugs to each of the older women in the congregation. He made "appointments" with his best friends to spend time with them.

Zain never told anyone, but he knew that it was time for saying good-bye and tying up loose ends. Monday morning he had a seizure. The CAT scan revealed that the tumor had grown so massively that it was a matter of days now until his death.

Kathy's hip recently had been broken, which caused her to be home constantly during those last weeks with Zain. Tuesday night she slept in a bed in another room in an attempt to keep her leg more comfortable. Zain asked if he could sleep with her. It was their last night together. They prayed, read, talked, slept, reminisced, laughed, and held each other through the night. It was God's gift to them. The next day Zain died in his parents' arms.

Several weeks after Zain's funeral, a dear eighty-four-year-old friend of Kathy asked her to come for lunch. She wanted to tell Kathy something that she never had told her before. She said that she had lost her four-year-old son in a drowning accident fifty years before, and that her grief hurt as much that day as it had the day it happened. She wanted Kathy to know that her pain would never stop—it would never "be over"—and that it was all right to hurt today, next year, or thirty years from now. Kathy was relieved and comforted. She would not have to feel guilty for carrying that pain with her when friends thought that she should be through grieving and go on with her life. There was no timetable for this deep grief. Kathy also knew that if she let that wound become calloused, her compassion for other hurting people would become calloused, too, and that would be the greatest tragedy of all.

One of the most helpful things that Kathy and David did through their last year together was to write letters to Zain in a journal. Kathy continued writing to him after his death. Zain was not dead but simply living in a new heavenly home. They have graciously allowed some of their journal entries to be printed here to teach helpers about the pains of grieving parents.

Dear Zain,

It's so strange—this strong feeling we all have that you lived your full life span. Too short for me but not for the Lord. He numbered your days before you were born, and you lived your complete life.

How can a boy twelve years old live a full life? But you did, and you did your job so well.

Love,
Mom

Dear Zain,

I admit I don't understand the "why" of what happened. But I don't have to, because I know our Lord, and I can accept it as part of his plan. He doesn't make mistakes. I trust him to know what he is doing and that it will serve a purpose (Rom. 8:28).

74

Too often we are so overwhelmed by the problem that we cannot see the purpose.

Love,
Mom

Dear Zain,

You love God and understand him in a more mature way than any other eleven-year-old I know. (And others see this in you as well.) God says he never gives us more than we can handle, and he's asked you to handle a lot . . . it's kind of like God saying, "Zain I trust you . . . with a very important job that I want you to do."

Zain, I believe that the important job God has trusted to you (and us with you) is to be a witness that will bring a lot of people to be saved.

There are so many who know you and are praying for you and you have a special place in their coming to know Jesus or growing stronger in *their* relationship with him. *What an important job*; what a special confidence God has in you. All because you (as all of our family) have put your confidence in him.

This is the day that the Lord has made, let us rejoice and be glad in Him.

Love,
Dad

Dear Zain,

One week ago we came home from spending the night at the hospital. Again they told us that the tumor had grown and that you had maybe a day, maybe a few months to live—just what they told us last year. Only this time, we knew in a different way that the end was truly near.

We called Mom and Grandpa and Grandma and Sister and told them but said too that life would go on. We made plans to get our Christmas tree and take me shopping in a wheelchair. You were so brave—you knew the tumor had grown, yet you didn't want to quit taking your medicines.

One week ago you came down about midnight and said you weren't real tired. One week ago you climbed in bed with me to spend your last night on earth with me.

It was such a special night. I knew that even then. I felt so gentle towards you and was so happy just to have you near. We talked for just a little while and then we both dozed off to sleep.

We awoke about two A.M. and talked some more. You were restless and I just talked to keep you calm. I asked if you wanted me to read to you as we always had, and you said yes.

I picked up the only book that looked at all fitting, *Once Upon a Summer* by Janette Oke. It talked about a twelve-year-old boy who was going through changes, changes he didn't really want but changes nonetheless. He wanted to go to his secret place that even his best friend didn't know—a place by a creek that was green and quiet. You said that you could even hear the bugs buzzing.

Then it talked of memories and how important they are—how you don't feel cheated if you have good memories. And so we started to talk about how neat it was to lie in bed and travel back through the last year and all the good memories: building bonfires after Christmas with Grandfather, finding peacock feathers in San Diego, going to the zoo with Jayne, holding baby Erin, swimming in the Pacific, making snowmen at Mt. Rose, winning Sir Fredrick at Circus-Circus, so many good memories. And we dozed off again.

76

We awoke again, and it was 6:41 A.M. I listened for your sister, Koran, and when I didn't hear her, I asked if you would go up and wake her—which you did. You seemed to be walking better, and I was glad.

You came back downstairs and climbed in again, and I think we thanked God for another day of being together. You asked me to get your school work for you. I turned and said, "Zain, I don't know why you have this tumor and I don't know why God is allowing it to grow again, but we won't give up. Right?"

And you beamed at me. "Right!"

A week ago Koran left for school. You started to have a headache and throw up. I had a doctor's appointment in Vallejo and decided to go. Daddy was here to be with you. John called and said Lawrence had died of a heart attack about one o'clock in the morning. I left for the appointment; everything took so long but I felt so calm. When I was finally there it was about 11:20, and I called Daddy to see what was happening. He said simply that he thought I had better come home, for you might not be with us much longer—that your time might have come.

Merr and I were calm. We went to the car, and I thanked God that Lawrence had died that day. It was such a comfort to know that he was there if you needed him. We prayed for you and cried a little. I remember telling Merr it was okay if she speeded a bit.

We got home, and you were on our bed. John had been here and prayed and cried and read Scripture with Dad.

We sat beside you and told you how we loved you and how proud we were of you. The hour passed quickly with lots of people calling. It seemed the phone never stopped ringing, but it wasn't an intrusion; instead it was like everyone was sending their love.

You always knew what we were saying to you. Oh, Babe, I miss you.

77

You had a kind of seizure. We held you and helped you to get comfortable. We told you to relax, and you did—more and more, until suddenly I knew you were no longer with us, even though you still breathed a few more times. I started to pray and asked Jesus to open the gates wide, and when I said *wide*, that was it—you were gone.

Then Dad prayed, then Merr. We sang and held you, Sandy, your dog, had her head on your leg. We cried—Daddy just like when Sarah died.

It didn't take long for you to cool down, and then I kissed you a last time. Sandy had already left. It was strange and neat, too, for she knew you—the person that she loved—was no longer in the world, and there was no reason for her to be there either.

Grandad and Grandma came; they knew you were already gone. Grandma said that when they were by Red Top she felt a peace and knew.

Koran came home and went in to see you. You were right not to have her be here—you loved her so.

John came back and helped us to call the mortuary. Suddenly it was four o'clock.

Justin came and went in and sat with you for a minute. That was hard for him, but I think it was the right thing.

The mortuary people came. Koran came in, and we hummed "Alleluia" together while they took you out. That was hard on both of us.

We were all calm; somehow it was supposed to be. Like Koran had said a year ago, "I don't know what's going to happen, but it will be okay." It was okay. The Lord had made it okay. He didn't solve our problem the way we wanted, but he surely did take away your tumor, and he had answered my prayers that you be as well as possible for as long as possible.

Here it is nine days later. . . . Christmas is ten days away, and we are leaving in a few hours to spend the weekend in Placerville like we'd planned. That was what was important to Koran—that we continue to do all the things we had planned on doing.

Your memorial service was beautiful, as you know. And it was so neat to feel like the Lord was giving me the words that each person needed to hear. I pray that that continues. We are going to plant the Zain Werum Memorial Forest at church. Right now we have three trees—Colorado blue spruces.

Beautiful trees made for boys.

Love,
Mom

Dear Zain,

This actually starts one week ago tonight. Thursday we were taking off for L.A., so Wednesday I had been up late finishing things. I went to bed, and the dull ache was here. I started to cry—the empty sob—just wanting you to be there to fill the void. Suddenly, before I really began, you were there. I wish I could remember exactly what you said, but the gist was that there was no need for me to feel lonely. You would always be near, and we would be together again.

I stopped crying—there was no need—and the feeling of you-do-"love-me-more" for you came back to comfort me. I know that was a selfless thing for you to do.

Throughout our trip I have felt you close. I only cried once, and that was at Disneyland watching the circus show (you loved it) and looking up at the beautiful cloudy sky and the two birds flying free overhead and thinking that you are free. I don't want to keep you shackled to me because I miss you so, for I love you more, too. I love you, Babe.

79

The joy of the Christian life is to be able to truly know that, whatever happens, we can truly be happy, for somehow it will fit into the Lord's plan.

Love,
Mom

Dear Zain,

It's been two months. . . .
Today I listened to the tape [of the funeral] for the first time. So good, and the quality is excellent, too.

This grief thing is strange; I *miss* you. I was conscious, this weekend in S.F., of just wanting to share with you, and feeling cheated because I can't. Also, I feel that it's unfair that you will always be "only" twelve years old in my mind. Thank goodness for our resurrection bodies.

Your sister got straight *A*s. I'm so proud. It's hard not to wonder how you would have done as a freshman.

I cried today and I feel better for it. I went through your room remembering how much you loved the things in it—the rocks, the marten on the rocks, each thing you placed there. You made the job so easy, because you had gone through so much already. Thank you.

I look at the places I failed you because of my own sin, and I'm sorry. I hope I didn't lead to your death. Lord forgive me.

Love,
Mom

Dear Zain,

I dreamed of you again—so vividly that you are still with me—walking and talking with you in the dream.

You were taller and older looking, yet still the same Zain. I'm not sure if you were trying to reassure me or yourself that you could still enjoy birthdays and holidays. . . .
    I miss you.

Love,
Mom

(written two and one-half years after Zain's death)

PART 3

The Long Journey After: Helping the Grieving Family

9

Helping After the Death

Now we come to the long journey after the death. The most effective helpers during bereavement are those who have supported the family through the diagnosis, hospitalization, and dying process. They have walked the entire road with them, and this sharing of their pain extends past the death into grief work. You, the helper, will be grieving, too. To cry with mourners is one of the most therapeutic gifts you can offer them. Yet, it is common for friends to distance themselves from the dying person and grieving family to protect themselves from pain. The helpers can experience the same isolation as the family if their friends see them as being too involved with the family.

The following "letter" is an integration of interviews with several grieving families, current research on grief and death, and my personal experience. It is designed to show what effectively helps the griever.

Dear Helper,

I have never known pain like this before. In losing my child, I have not only lost my dear loved one, I have lost a part of myself. I her mother carried that child inside of me for nine months. She will always be a part of me. Holding her in my arms for the first time was a time of joy. Holding her for the last time is a time of grief and sorrow. I her father cherished this child as my heritage and my future hope.

I am physically and emotionally exhausted from caring for my dying child. It was a full-time job that consumed me. There was room for nothing else in our lives—not even our marriage. Our relationship has deteriorated. Our savings are gone. Our careers have suffered; how could we concentrate? We had to take excessive time off work.

Then there was the guilt. When I was at home with my other children, I felt guilty for not being at the hospital. When I was at the hospital with my dying child, I felt guilty for leaving my other children. I couldn't win. It tore me apart.

The hospital was my lifeline. The staff became my friends. I relied on being with other families going through the same ordeal. I became attached to other patients—my child's friends. Now I no longer belong there. Where do I belong? I have lost my role.

There is a good reason for the term *grief work*. Grieving a loved one is hard work. When the shock wears off, my grief work will require every ounce of concentration and energy that I have. You cannot do it for me, but you can stand by to grieve with me. I must fully embrace this grief or I will never be healed from it.

Physically I will struggle: not feel well, not eat, sleep, or care for my physical body. Those tasks seem very petty now. Do bring me meals so that I have the chance to eat. I do need nourishment and strength, though I don't enjoy eating. I am just numb.

Please do not advise me, impose what you think best for me, or judge how I am grieving. Everyone grieves differently, in different time frames in different ways. Remember that I am still the "same person." My temperament has not changed. If I have always been an extrovert, socially active, and gained strength from being with groups of people, I will need my friends around me now more than ever. But if I have been a private, introverted person who gained perspective in solitude, please don't decide that I shouldn't be alone now. I will need my privacy to work through this. Of course, I will still need people, just as the extrovert will need some time alone. But take your cue from me. Ask me what I want and respect it.

When you are with me, love me, hold me, cry with me. Feel my hurt in your heart. Pray for me with tears. Let me feel God's love and care for me through you, and Jesus' arms around me through yours. Understand that I must move through the stages of grief: shock, denial, anger, guilt, and depression. I will have disturbing dreams. It may take a few weeks or a few years for me

87

to go through this. Most parents enter this grief process when they first learn of their child's terminal illness.

Above all, *Listen to me*. Let me tell you that "this isn't happening to me"; let me be angry at God and everyone around me; allow me to wonder aloud if the death is my fault. Be my safe place to talk and cry and feel totally accepted. I need my lifeline of friends now.

Please do not make trite, insensitive statements such as these: "Time heals all wounds," "I know how you feel," "Everything will be all right," "God will not give you more than you can bear," "At least you have three other children." Please do not tell me about someone else's story that is sadder than mine or send me books on grief. Don't say or do anything to minimize my grief. This only says that you have no idea how deeply I am hurting.

Please do come and share a relevant passage of Scripture with me as part of our relationship based in unconditional love. But do not quote Scripture out of context *at* me with no effort made to love me first. This is the "Scripture wall" used by Christians who need to feel that they have done their duty without having invested time in a relationship. Jesus never did that, and I need to see Jesus now.

Help me to be fully involved in the funeral. I want to celebrate my child's life. It was short, but worth living. Let me plan this as my last gift for my child. Understand that the funeral is not really for my child; it is for us who have been left behind. It is a time for tribute, for good-byes. I need to be active in this. It is an event that I will cherish always. Well-meaning friends sometimes take over every detail of the funeral to spare the griever's pain. Sometimes they even clean out the room of the deceased so that the griever will not have to face it. You cannot spare me this pain, so do not try. I have to walk through every memory and relive our life together. I must look at every picture in every scrapbook, touch every toy, see the half-done homework, hear her favorite songs, etc. Let me be immersed in my grief. I must create something out of this grief—write a journal, compile a scrapbook of bereavement cards, compose a song or poetry, paint, or whatever God puts in my heart to do. I must have an outlet. That's what David did in the Psalms.

Encourage me to walk this road of reviewing the life we and our child had together. Take over the practical chores for me (washing, cleaning, cooking, transporting our other children) so that I have time to grieve.

Realize that our marriage is struggling now. It is not true that "crisis brings people together" when a dying child is involved. One partner (usually the wife) wants to talk about the death, while the other (usually the husband) wants to avoid the topic. The pain is too deep. Marriages are strained. We are probably grieving in different ways, in different time frames, and this is ripping us apart. Do not expect us to be the same couple you knew.

If you can, put me in touch with other people who have lost their children—when I am ready. There is no empathy like that of someone who has had a similar experience. I may want to belong to a support group, or have only one fellow sufferer to share with.

Don't tell me that "God is preparing me for a great ministry." I'm sure that this is true, but I am not ready to hear it yet. I can barely get out of bed, much less help someone else. This is also not a time for a discussion of doctrine. Whether you believe in God's total control or you believe in free choice and the consequences of sin on earth, your revelation of God's will for my life may be true, but it will not comfort me. My survival will come from completely focusing on my relationship with God through Jesus Christ. Help me focus on his tender, fatherly care of me and on Jesus' victory even in death. Don't distract me with figuring out God's plan. The most comforting thing you can say is, "I don't understand, but I love you and I'll be here." His love and presence—those are the promises of God. Reflect them to me.

Don't avoid the subject of my deceased child. Don't avoid his name in conversation as if he never existed. That is very painful to me. You can say, "Tommy would have liked that," "That would have made Jenny laugh," "That was Sally's favorite ice cream." I am already thinking it, so give me an opening to talk about it.

Stand by me when I try to reenter the mainstream of life. Go with me on that first supermarket trip. Be there when I see my child's favorite cereal.

You must understand that the hardest part of my grief comes after the funeral and the initial few months have passed. This is when the support of people around me will begin to diminish. Life must go on for them as well as for me, but I'm not finished grieving. Please remember us on the following days:

our child's birthday

the date of his/her death

holidays (especially Christmas, Mother's/Father's Day)

any days that you know were special to us as a family

The first year's anniversaries are the hardest to bear. As the years go on, the pain will decrease, but it will always be there. Don't forget us.

Please remember my other children. Do special things for them now. Talk with them; love them; listen to their fears. Help me parent them. I have to say good-bye to one child before I can be a whole parent again.

Someday, but *not* in the early stages, I will need outlets of exercise, hobbies, and new interests to fill the time, distract me from pain, and find new purpose. Don't push me, but be there to encourage me when I'm ready.

Don't wait for me to be "my old self." Losing my child has changed me forever. Fifty years from now, my grief will still be with me.

Love,
The Griever

Summary

In summary, then, always try to do and keep in mind the following:

1. Grieving is hard work.
2. Understand that the stages of grief are normal: shock, physical symptoms, denial, anger, guilt,

depression, acceptance of death, hope to continue. But be aware that there is no textbook formula for the grief process. Everyone moves through the stages in different orders, time frames, and degrees of intensity.

3. Respect the wishes of grievers, and do not assume that you "know what's best for them" based on your experience.

4. Provide an environment of unconditional love, acceptance, and listening.

5. Do not minimize the unique pain and grief of each mourner.

6. Mirror God's love and scriptural truth in Jesus Christ; do not "preach" it.

7. Help the griever to be fully involved in the funeral planning.

8. Support those who grieve as they review their child's life to the last detail.

9. Encourage them to find a creative outlet for their pain. Supply them with needed tools.

10. Do tangible chores such as bringing meals and providing transportation. *You* take care of all the loose ends.

11. Be sensitive to the strain on the marriage and the needs of the siblings. Provide a listening ear to the siblings when it is too painful for the parents to fill that role initially.

12. Be a link to other grievers who have experienced the death of a child. Have information about support groups in the area for those who are interested.

13. Talk about the deceased child. Cry and mourn with the griever.
14. Do not forget the family after the "initial accepted mourning period" passes. Remember specific anniversary dates in their lives, especially the child's birth date and date of death.
15. Be available to support the extended family— grandparents, aunts, uncles, and others. They must grieve, too, and will not want to burden the grieving parents.

From a Chaplain's View: Followup After the Death

In closing this chapter, I present the excellent bereavement followup program developed by Gerald Hill at Mt. Diablo Hospital, Concord, California. This should provide you with a model for developing your own followup program.

Monthly letters are sent to families who have lost a loved one at the hospital. These letters remind families that they are not forgotten or alone. Relevant topics are covered, such as dealing with grief at holiday time. Available support groups are listed.

Bereavement support groups are offered in eight-week series. The focus of the group is to encourage members to share their stories of loss and hear others'. Each week a different theme on grief sets the stage. Groups are organized according to the type of loss. Widows meet in a group. Parents who have lost a child meet in another. Children who have lost a parent or sibling can attend their own bereavement group. Ongoing support groups are available for those interested after the series is finished.

Grief counseling is also offered on an individual basis. This program interfaces with the chemical dependency and psychiatric units. Obviously, chemically dependent and emotionally ill people have added trouble resolving grief and require more intense therapy.

Workshops on grief and loss are offered as community services to the public in churches, schools, and community centers. Preparation and prevention are relevant for all of us.

The themes which the support series covers include:

What is the grief process?
Is it normal to feel what I'm feeling?
What should I do when the pain seems too great?
What thoughts and feelings can I expect?
What can I learn from grief?
How do I take care of myself?
How can I cope with holidays and anniversaries?
How do I begin to reinvest in life?
What resources are available?
What about making major decisions?
What kind of support do I need?

10

Surviving the Unbearable: More Advice from the Experts

The following account is of a very special journey toward regaining God's hope after enduring the dark tunnel. It also is an excellent example of how parents can best help siblings to cope with their loss.

Karen's life had always overflowed with God's goodness. Raised in a loving Christian home, she had enjoyed a genuine faith in Jesus Christ since she was a young child. A deep trust in God and desire to obey him marked Karen's life. Now she was a beautiful woman with a dedicated husband, a set of seven-year-old twin girls, Sarah and Michelle, a four-year-old son, and another baby due shortly. Karen was a talented pianist who gave generously of her gifts to the church and taught music in her home. She had decided against pursuing further opportunities in music to be a dedicated wife and mother. Her husband and children were the joy of her life—especially Sarah.

Sarah was extremely bright, active, loving, affectionate—a very special little girl. She was good at everything, did well in school and gymnastics, and was also her mother's star piano student. She had a motherly touch, was protective of her sister and brother, and was kind to everyone around her. She brought joy to all.

Sarah had always been very healthy, but one summer's day Karen decided that Sarah should see the doctor about her cold. The doctor informed Karen that Sarah had a cancerous tumor growing in her chest area. A biopsy would need to be done immediately. The good news was that there was an 80 percent chance of recovery from this type of cancer. There was hope.

Karen and Steve were encouraged. God had always protected them and he would show his power in protecting Sarah now. The doctors said that they could do the biopsy at the local hospital, and Sarah could go right home.

But Sarah never went home. The doctor failed to use the correct pediatric-size tube. Sarah's trachea collapsed, she went into convulsive breathing and cardiac arrest and then into a coma. Even if she came out of the coma, she would have severe brain damage.

Sarah was rushed to the intensive care unit of the nearest children's hospital. The doctors there verified that if the procedure had been done at the children's hospital with specialized pediatric equipment, Sarah would have been fine.

Karen and Steve went home to tell their two children, who adored Sarah, that she would not be coming home. Life had to go on. Karen was about to give birth to a new baby. Steve had a new job and was also in school. How could God have done this to his faithful followers? Life was unraveling, and the questions were deafening.

Sarah's specialists started her on chemotherapy and radiation for the cancer. Though family members were at her bedside around the clock, Sarah was never to come out of her coma.

The first day of school was the hardest moment in the whole ordeal for Karen. She had to take Michelle to school without her twin and protector, Sarah, and face the questions of the staff: "Where is Sarah? Isn't she coming today?" The pain was crushing.

Timothy, Karen and Steve's second son, was born three weeks later. With the demands of a new infant, Karen could not visit Sarah as often as she wanted. Michelle and her brother had visited Sarah to talk to her and hold her. Now it was Timothy's turn. Karen placed him in Sarah's arms. He would never know this sister.

To add to the pain, Karen and Steve and some of their extended family were actively part of a church that believed strongly in healing. Karen and Steve believed in healing. Yes, God *would* heal Sarah. But four months after the onset of the coma, Sarah's doctor called a family conference. Sarah's condition was worsening; she was dying. The doctor recommended stopping the cancer treatments. The end had come. Karen and Steve were faced with the toughest decision of their lives. One side of their family said that God would still heal Sarah. She should be kept alive in any fashion. The other side of the family said that perhaps God had already taken Sarah from them and they should accept it.

Karen and Steve painfully came to the realization that their precious Sarah was dying; it was time to let her go. Members of the church opposed their decision and sent prayer teams twenty-four hours a day to her hospital bedside. They were unable to minister to Karen and Steve, but they could pray for healing. Karen had the painful task of asking that they stop, because the nurses' and doctors' care of Sarah was being disrupted. The chaos was not good for Sarah.

Sarah died that week. Not only did Karen and Steve have to face their own intense grief and their children's grief, they also faced a broken relationship with their church. Even members of their own extended family were angry with them and accused them of not being Christians.

Where was God? Where was his presence? Where were his loving, protective arms? They had lost their daughter and now they had lost their Christian support system. They had survived pain upon pain upon pain for months. God had been with them through the funeral and first hard month, but now their faith was crumbling and the darkness was engulfing them. If their Bible-based belief in healing and God's protection was untrue, then what was true? The questions and doubts flooded in. Karen and Steve entered a dark tunnel of examining every aspect of their faith and relationship with God.

But God never abandons us. He promises to be with his children, even into the "valley of the shadow of death." Though we do not "feel" him, God constantly works for our good. He would lead Karen and Steve through the dark tunnel.

Karen's precious new son was a great source of joy and comfort. Karen desperately missed her role of mothering Sarah, but nurturing and caring for their new baby helped to fill her empty arms and heart.

God gave Karen a determination to rebuild a life for her husband and three children. When severe depression came, and she needed to talk, she could reach out to her parents and sister, who were very supportive and always willing to listen. Karen and Steve also realized that physical activity is the best weapon against depression. They immersed themselves in a construction project on their home, and Karen exercised regularly in an aerobics class. Though their marriage was rock solid, the strains and feelings of guilt common to grieving parents were unavoidable. Karen needed to talk about her pain, but Steve couldn't bear to hear Sarah's name mentioned; the pain was too deep. They finally compromised by talking about Sarah's good times. Karen would talk to friends about the sad times.

Karen stopped teaching piano. Since music touches the deepest parts of our emotions, it is either a great comfort or it is unbearable. Because Karen was a musician and through Sarah she had had hope for continuing her music-related dreams, the associations were intensely painful. It was time for Karen to take a break from her music and focus completely on supporting her family. Friends came to help with meals and household chores, which freed Karen to spend time with her children. Michelle was their child who had suffered most from Sarah's death. Michelle had not lost a sibling as her brother had; Michelle had lost her other half. A twin-sister relationship is the closest of all sibling relationships. Karen understood this and stepped in to be Michelle's partner and spend most of her time with her.

Karen and Steve had done an excellent job of helping their children cope with Sarah's death. They had always been honest and never kept secrets from them. They included their children in every aspect of the loss. They took them to say good-bye to Sarah at her bedside after her death and helped them to attend the funeral. Following the funeral, they left on a week-long retreat to gain perspective as a new family.

Karen and Steve continued to talk about Sarah, but they were careful not to idolize her or transfer their dreams for Sarah onto Michelle.

Though Karen and Steve had lost their church home, they were still a part of "God's church." God sent a host of Christians from various denominations from the community to support them. Sarah and Michelle's public school was the most consistent, loving source of support. Karen felt most helped by fellow Christians who had suffered similar tragedies and came to put their arms around her, cry with her, and listen to her.

Karen and Steve survived their year's journey through the dark tunnel. Eventually they resolved the broken relationship with their church but never returned there as members. They now attend another church. Today Karen and Steve stand as rocks of true faith and compassionate ministers. When other grieving Christians ask them, "How could God do this to me?" Karen and Steve can say, "We don't understand, either. We miss Sarah desperately, and it will always hurt. But we will travel this road with you. You will survive the darkness and return to a life of faith. We did."

11

Special Situations

The focus of this book is the terminally ill child, and the purpose is to guide those who help the child and family through hospitalization and death. Helpers must be aware of the spectrum of death's possibilities. Many times you will be called to work with mourning families in situations where you never had the opportunity to work with the child. Death comes by catastrophic accident, murder, abduction, suicide, miscarriage, stillbirth, or sudden infant death syndrome. Aging parents may lose an adult child by death. Whether the child was a fifty-year-old son supporting his parents or was lost after three months in the womb, the child is *dead,* and the pain and grief are the same for the parents. Even the mother who aborts her baby, who chooses for her child to die, endures post abortion syndrome, a very real grieving process intensified by severe guilt. You must treat each family's grief with the same empathy and tenderness, never judging the severity of the grief in relation to its circumstances.

Miscarriages

Parents who have no children and desperately want them are totally crushed when the wife miscarries. They lose their unborn child and their dream of parenthood. A mother with other children who miscarries is just as pained. She knows what she has lost, because she has held other babies in her arms. She grieves the loss of a sibling for her children and must deal with their sorrow. *A miscarriage is a death*. The helper must never minimize the situation by saying, "But you have other children"; "You will have other children"; "It must have been best for the baby, or God wouldn't have taken it."

Kristi and her husband with their three-year-old daughter had just moved to a different part of the state when Kristi conceived their second child. They had no friends, yet, nor a church home, and Kristi was very lonely. Her pregnancy was a great comfort to her, signifying the start of a new life in a new town. When she miscarried, she was devastated and had no support system of friends to turn to. A distant friend, Ann, in a nearby city heard of Kristi's dilemma and sprang into action. Ann asked her church to pray for Kristi and then came herself every day to cook, clean, and watch Kristi's daughter as Kristi recovered. Other women from Ann's church began calling and offering help. Kristi felt totally loved by a church body she had never met.

Though Kristi and her husband had had serious marriage struggles in the past, he was now a solid source of comfort for her. This is not uncommon. While the death of a child strains a marriage, many wives who miscarry find their most supportive friends to be their husbands. Critical to the woman's ability to cope with the loss is that her husband be involved and share her grief.

Kristi conceived and delivered a healthy baby one year later. It was the greatest cure for her loss. To this day she tells her children that they have a sister or brother in heaven who is a part of their family. But those women who never have another baby after the miscarriage carry the pain with them indefinitely.

Virginia[1] suffered five miscarriages. She and her husband, Ron, had been trying for a year to conceive a child when she became pregnant. They were thrilled and then equally devastated when she lost their first baby. It wasn't until after her second miscarriage that the doctor discovered she had fibroid tumors. Following surgery, she conceived and gave birth to a healthy baby girl. They adored their precious gift and wanted to give her a sibling. Three more miscarriages followed. The last miscarriage required a hysterectomy, which ended the dream of having another child.

Each miscarriage was painful, but the one following the birth of their daughter was the most difficult. The baby was over three months along, and Virginia heard the heartbeat. Two days later she went in for her routine amniocentesis. After starting the procedure, the staff immediately left the room for discussion. The baby was dead. Virginia's doctor hoped that the baby would naturally abort, preventing more surgery. Two weeks later the baby had not aborted, and Virginia still carried the dead child inside her. The emotional pain was unbearable. She lashed out in anger toward everyone. After she became angry with her daughter her guilt would be overwhelming. She was on an emotional roller coaster until the doctor finally removed the baby.

Virginia's husband and daughter were her source of comfort and healing. Ron was torn up inside and had a deep feeling of helplessness as he watched his wife hurt emotionally and physically but was unable to relieve her pain. Friends who would simply be there to listen to Virginia were very helpful. Virginia's husband held an informal service in their home for the family to say good-bye to the baby. But Virginia still carries the grief of losing that child with her.

When a child is stillborn or dies shortly after birth, the parents can grieve more openly than over a miscarriage. They can hold the dead baby and create memories that will comfort them in later years. They can be involved in planning a funeral and saying good-bye to their infant. It is important that helpers remember the "birth date/death date" in years to come. But the helper should never underestimate the severity of the parents' grief following the loss of either an unborn child or an infant.

Catastrophic Accidents

The catastrophic-accident death causes the most difficult grief to bear. The parents of the terminally ill child begin grieving when they learn of the illness. They have a time of preparation and are able to say good-bye to their child when he or she is still alive. They already have moved through some of the stages of grief work and are nearer to acceptance when the death arrives.

When a child dies in a catastrophic accident, the parents have no preparation and are in shock. It will take them months and years to move through grief work. The most painful part of the ordeal is never having had a chance to say good-bye or create those needed last memories.

Helen and her family always vacationed at their second home in Sun Valley, Idaho. Their two sons loved the outdoors and mountain life, and this area was the ideal retreat from the stressful executive job that Helen's husband, Matt, held in California. Thanksgiving arrived, and Helen, Matt, and their ten-year-old son, Steven, headed for their vacation home. Thirteen-year-old Paul was remaining at home with friends to participate in a band concert.

Duck hunting season in Idaho was in full swing. Matt and his best friend, both expert outdoorsmen, decided to take Steven duck hunting with them. When they did not return by nightfall, Helen became concerned, but she trusted her husband's abilities in the wild. Later that night, the community organized a search party. The next morning Matt, his friend, and Steven were found frozen to death by the lake. The cause would always be a mystery. What had gone wrong? Had Steven fallen into the lake? Had the men rescued him and then perished in the freezing temperatures? No one would ever know what actually happened.

Helen's pain was overwhelming. Losing her life's partner was devastating; but losing her precious younger
son was even less bearable, and she had no husband
to turn to for help. How would she tell Paul that the
father he adored and the brother he loved were both
gone? She was enveloped in numbness and shock for
weeks.

Helen and Matt had many dear friends in Idaho as
well as California. They never left her side. She and her
husband had always been very social people. Their lives
had been filled with activity. She did *not* want to be
alone now. Friends chartered a plane and went back
with her to California. Friends met her at the plane and
brought her home where relatives were already staying. Helen needed people to surround her. Years later,
she still did not want to be alone.

Helen and Paul survived the funeral with the support
of numerous friends. The two caskets side-by-side—
one large, one so small in contrast—were the painful
focus of the service.

Paul reacted to the deaths in a way typical of
teenagers. He wanted to go to school the next day. He
immersed himself in constant activities to numb the
pain. He would not cry in front of his mother and
became angry when she cried. Helen would have to
hide her pain from Paul. He could not handle one more
burden.

Their first Christmas alone, only a few weeks after
the deaths, was the saddest holiday they would spend.
Helen could not bear to have their traditional Christmas
at home. She even refused to have a Christmas tree.

Paul was adamant that they must have a tree, and a group of his high school friends came to help him decorate it. Helen and Paul left to spend Christmas Day with Helen's brother's family in another city, something they had never done before. Paul felt totally betrayed. Not only had he lost his family, but now he had lost all his family's traditions.

Over the years, Helen and Paul pieced their lives back together. Paul went on a journey of searching, which eventually brought him to a genuine faith in Jesus Christ. Helen remarried a wonderful man who had been a dear friend of Matt's—the same man who had met Matt's and Steven's bodies at the airport when they arrived for the funeral. Each year her new husband sent Helen a dozen red roses on Steven's birthday. He wanted her to know that Steven and Matt would never be forgotten.

The most comforting fact that helpers can communicate to grieving families is that the helpers will not forget the lost loved ones but will help keep their love and traditions alive.

Losing Adult Children

Ninety-nine-year-old Mary was often visited in the senior facility where she lived by her favorite son, Tom. Though her body was failing, her mind was as sharp as ever. Tom was her lifeline. He and his sons were a constant source of joy for her. The hardest thing that Mary's grandson ever had to do was tell Mary that her sixty-nine-year-old child, Tom, was dead. He had died in a tragic suicide. Mary never asked how he died, and the family respected this as her way of indicating that she did not need to know.

Mary attended the funeral in a state of shock. How difficult it must have been for her to endure the next week, which held both Mother's Day and Tom's birthday. He had been a most wonderful Mother's Day present almost seventy years before. A few weeks later Mary required surgery on an ulcer and suffered a stroke. She died soon after. The family realized that Mary had given up any will to live. Without Tom there was no reason to keep fighting for life.

When an adult dies, helpers tend to focus their support on the immediate family—the deceased's spouse and children. People often forget that the deceased has parents who must deal with the loss of their child. Probably the parents are aging, and the child was not only their son or daughter but had changed roles and become their primary support.

I made regular visits to an aging woman in our church a few years ago. Though she was ill and dying, had a dedicated husband who was mourning her coming death, and had other caring children, she was completely focused on the death of her adult son, which had occurred decades earlier. He had been killed in a shooting accident, and the pain of losing him still far exceeded any present pain that she endured.

Helpers must remember that many aging parents lose children. Their grief is as intense as that of parents of young children, but their options for coping with the pain are more limited. When any human being dies, whether a child in the womb or a sixty-year-old adult, remember to ask, "Who are the grieving parents?"

Fred and Carol Patterson have graciously allowed the accounts they wrote of their adult daughter's death to be printed here. Ten years ago Fred and Carol were planning their twenty-fifth wedding anniversary party. They had much to celebrate—their marriage, their friends, the two beautiful grown daughters they had raised, their treasured grandchildren, and countless rich blessings of God. They attended not an anniversary party that week but a funeral.

Human beings deceive themselves into believing that they can control parts of their lives. Fred and Carol teach us that what is most important in life hangs by a fragile thread, held only by God.

A Father's Grief

When the phone rang, I groggily answered, and someone was saying, "Fred—this is Yvonne [my son-in-law's sister]. Now, don't panic, but there was a wreck. Sarah and Ryan are fine. Lori and Brian were injured and are being treated at Marshall Hospital. But Lori is being transferred to the U.C. hospital in Sacramento." My heart sank as my mind raced through all the possible results.

Then a calm clutched my mind, and God gave me his word: "There are no ifs"—if they hadn't left so tired, if they hadn't left so early, etc. "If" is hindsight of how we think God should have handled things.

I related everything to Carol, and I could see her mind trying to comprehend the little information we had. I told her there were no ifs. We wrapped our arms around each other and prayed. While Carol was getting dressed, I called all the godly men I knew: our pastor, former pastors, deacons, leaders in the church, and other friends. I simply said, "Lori and Brian have been in a wreck and are in the hospital. Please pray." I didn't reach everyone, but I knew that as soon as they heard about what happened, they would be praying.

When we arrived at the hospital, we were escorted to a waiting room. After a while, an intern liaison came in and told us, "Lori has a torn liver, which was operated on at Marshall Hospital. She received a hard blow to the head, which has caused her brain to swell, but they drilled a hole in her skull to relieve the pressure. She is having a CAT scan now to see how much swelling there is and then will be taken to her room where you can see her."

Our hopes soared at the supposed "good" news. I hung onto God's "no ifs." But Lori never regained consciousness. I have never seen so many tubes, bags, and machines hooked up to anyone. We talked to her, even though she couldn't respond. I kept telling her that Brian and the kids were okay.

We were all worn out by the fourth day. Lori was all puffy and looked like a balloon. I held her hand and told her that Brian and the kids were okay. She squeezed my hand, and I heard (and felt) her in my heart say, "It's all right, Dad. I love you, and I know they are okay, and everything will be fine. God is in charge."

I told the doctor who was present that Lori had squeezed my hand. He looked at me in a condescending way and said, "I don't think so—it was probably just a muscle spasm." It wasn't until then that I knew she was dead, and they were just following the routine of waiting for her brain to die. With all his education, this doctor thought he had the scientific answers, but he overlooked the power of God. God can do all things, including raising the dead to say good-bye.

We were asked to leave the room, and a short time later the doctors came out to tell us that Lori had died. We all gathered in a huddle and cried and sobbed. The quarterback, Jesus, was still in charge, calling all the plays in our lives.

Carol and I almost felt guilty for not falling apart. But we knew that God, in his wonderful mercy, gave us "a peace beyond human understanding."

The church was packed for the memorial service. Everyone at the service came to express their condolences to us at our front-row pew. Our Christian family was so kind and had many wonderful things to say. Some were so shaken that we were ministering to them. I think the greatest compliment, and glory to our Jesus, came from people who said it was more like a marriage than a memorial service.

We praise God for our wonderful daughters. Lori and Susan were gifts from him, and we dedicated them to him when they were babies. I am not an Abraham who has such faith to place Isaac on the altar and sacrifice him (my daughters) by my own hand, but I'll tell you what—God is sufficient in *all* things.

113

We thank God that he spared Brian, Sarah, and Ryan. The car rolled three or four times and came to rest on its side, with Brian halfway out the door. One more roll probably would have killed Brian. He was sore and needed twenty stitches to the back of his head. The babies (seven months and nineteen months old) didn't have a scratch. To the unsaved this seemed to be quite a coincidence. But for those of us who love Jesus and have experienced his intervention know he is the truth and the light, and our lives are in his hands.

A Mother's Grief

Our daughter Lori, her husband Brian, and children Sarah and Ryan left our home about 4:30 A.M. following a weekend visit with us on June 28, 1982. Baby Ryan had been fussy most of the night. Since our daughter was already awake with the baby, she decided it would be best to begin their trip home. Brian had to be home in time to clean up to be at work by 8:00 A.M.

We hugged and kissed everyone good-bye as Brian drove off with his little family. We wished them a safe trip home, as we always did, and went back in the house to try to get a couple more hours of sleep before beginning our own demanding jobs.

The phone rang around 6:30 A.M. I was a little concerned when the phone rang in our quiet bedroom so early in the morning. My husband, Fred, answered the call. This was very unusual, because he usually left the phone calls for me to answer. I'm sure the Lord planned it this way.

As soon as Fred started talking, I knew something was very wrong. My heart began to pound, my mouth became dry, and a huge lump came into my throat.

"The kids have been in an auto accident," Brian's sister was saying. "The children appear to be okay. Brian has a bad cut to his head and they are sewing it up. His shoulder and arm are also injured but don't appear to be broken. Lori is in emergency surgery, and due to a head injury, has to be transferred from the Marshall Hospital to the University of Davis Medical Center in Sacramento." This sounded serious. I began a silent prayer.

We learned later that our daughter had offered to drive the last half of the trip home so Brian could get a little extra sleep before he had to go to work. This precious little family got within nine miles of home when our daughter apparently fell asleep at the wheel. The car hit a guard rail on the freeway, causing the car to flip over several times. Lori was the only one thrown partially out of the car. She wasn't wearing a seatbelt! She had the most severe injuries. The children surely had a guardian angel looking over them as Sarah, nineteen months old, was only in an infant seat, and Ryan, seven months, was lying on a pillow asleep on the back seat. Both children were only sore and slightly bruised. There was no human reason the children should have survived. Thank you, Jesus.

As soon as Fred hung up the phone, we hugged each other and prayed. Then Fred started making phone calls to all the "prayer warriors" we knew. After that, we headed for the hospital.

Only a parent who has seen a child (a grown woman of twenty-four but *still our child*) lying in a bed in a coma with obvious severe injuries can know how we felt at that moment. The tears began to flow. Over the next four days there were a lot of tears and fervent prayers.

We learned from a staff social worker that Lori had a severe injury to her head and spine. She was paralyzed from the waist down and remained in a coma. It didn't look good. We kept praying.

On the fourth day following the accident, severe swelling of the brain occurred and couldn't be controlled. Our dear, sweet daughter was gone.

I just couldn't believe it. How could this be? She was only twenty-four years old. She had two small babies to raise. She was a beautiful Christian woman.

Fred and I turned to the Lord for help and comfort. Our ever-present loving Lord was there for us as always. Praise God. At that moment God lifted us above the present situation and held us there through the next several trying days.

We began making phone calls, thanking our friends in Christ for their prayers and support, letting them know that God had allowed Lori to "go home."

Lori was a loving and giving person and was loved in return by young and old alike. She was "in love with love" and had been since she was a little girl. She had spent hours writing poetry and singing. Lori married her high school sweetheart and had two children. All her dreams had come true. She was a loving Christian woman and knew the Lord in a personal way.

On July 6, 1982, the day after our twenty-fifth wedding anniversary, we had a memorial service for our daughter.

What a blessing that service was! Over two hundred friends and family attended. The service was filled with music, beautiful flowers, and a lot of Christian love. The Lord gave us the strength, comfort, and peace to greet each dear family and friend present. The service was full of joy and made everything begin to make some sense.

We know God has a plan and purpose for *everything* that comes into our lives. So we did accept Lori's death, knowing one day we will see the whole picture clearly.

Many hearts were touched during that memorial service. Over the weeks following the service we learned of several who had rededicated their lives to Christ, marriages that were strengthened, parents who felt a deeper love and appreciation for their children, and an overall awareness of how suddenly our lives here on earth can be changed.

We continually thank God for giving us two beautiful Christian daughters. Our daughter Susan was a great blessing to us during those difficult days and the months that followed. We were able to be a comfort to each other.

Following our daughter's memorial service, and after much prayer and discussion with our son-in-law, we decided it would be best for our grandchildren to be brought home to live with us until better arrangements could be made. We all agreed that these precious little ones would be much better off staying with Gramma and Grampa all day while Daddy worked than in a day-care center. The babies spent the weeks with us and most weekends with their daddy. The days and weeks went by.

We had the privilege of raising our grandchildren for one and a half years. Then Brian remarried. He and his new wife, Janeene, were able to bring the children home to once again be a family unit. Brian and Janeene have added a daughter, Janell, to their family, and we love them all.

Because of our love for our grandchildren and our full-time devotion to them over that year and a half, we truly did not have time to grieve. We put it on hold for several years. We definitely do not recommend doing this. No matter what the circumstances, there is always a period of grieving. Without living it we cannot have a normal time of healing. Not until nine years later were we able to release the deep sorrow and emptiness we felt for our daughter and carried in our hearts. We will miss her until we meet again in heaven.

The greatest blessing in my life came four years after the death of our daughter. I had turned to the Lord for a healing of my broken heart and financial problems. At the very moment I came to him, the Lord showed himself to me in his physical form. Praise God! I saw every detail of our blessed Jesus down to the well-worn robe and sandals he was wearing. The sandals showed many miles of walking with worn leather on the outer straps. Then the Lord looked at me with the largest eyes you have ever seen, so full of love and compassion, far more than I could ever share or capture in words. All I know is that the love that shone in his eyes will never leave me. And his arms appeared long and wrapped around and around me, assuring me all the while that he would always be there to comfort me. Thank you, Jesus, for giving me a blessing that will last a lifetime.

You see, even out of tragedy the Lord will give us an abundant blessing. We only need come unto him and ask.

12

Helpers or Judges?

Deaths that bring the deepest grief and pain of all are those of dying persons who feel they are "unacceptable." As one griever put it, "If my brother was dying from a brain tumor, I would feel comfortable telling anyone, confident of immediate sympathy and support. But telling people, especially Christians, that my brother is dying of AIDS and that he lived a homosexual lifestyle . . . that brings a very different initial response, one of shock and questions."

In this chapter are two such stories. One woman graciously allowed me to print her letter about her son's murder, if names were changed. Another griever has written the story of her family helping her brother as he died from AIDS and grieving his death.

Both young men lived lifestyles opposed to biblical principles. Yet, would any compassionate Christian *really* believe that these children "deserved what they got"? No one can help hurting people as they die or comfort their grieving families who does not grasp the fact that no one sin is bigger than any other. Imagine that we could contract a fatal disease from gossiping, backbiting, bitterness, lying, arrogance, pride, impatience—or judging others. Everyone who is without Jesus falls short of the glory of God. Christ did not come to heal perfect people.

My Son Was Murdered

Dear Mary Ann:

I have given a lot of thought to writing a chapter about my son's murder for your book, but I must decline.

There are several reasons for this, but two are the strongest and the ones that swayed my decision the most: (1) negative feelings about the idea from my husband, and the fact that some of Tom's brothers and sisters still have not dealt fully with the loss; and (2) the fact that his death is an unsolved homicide and it could become an active file if something new came up, which could engender new feelings and all kinds of problems.

Because I'm a writer by nature, I did give the idea a lot of thought, and if I were the only one to be considered, it would be done. The areas of focus would be that there is an extra kind of pain involved when the death is sudden, and another element is added when it is public and "notorious" in its own way. Tom was not living the lifestyle we would have preferred at the time of his death. But murder generates newspaper articles that aren't always positive/correct, and both seem to attract people who want to know details rather than share pain—which can add to the pain. But the other side of that is the wonderful, incredible, and tremendously healing realization that God himself knew the very same pain we did. His own Son was murdered, too. That thought was awesome, in the true sense of that word, to me.

If we are Christians, death should not be looked at as the awful end, but rather as a temporary separation. Tom had received Christ as a teenager, and I trust in the promises connected with that. The fact that I know I'll see him again was/is a big part of the healing process for me. I really am not concerned about "who" or "why," except that it would bring closure to the situation and ease some of the pain of others in the family. Knowing "who" or "why" can't bring him back, and there is always the awful possibility out there that "who" is someone else's child.

Although I can talk and write easily about Tom, I often do so with tears that remain very close to the surface. There is strong emotion wrapped up in his life and his death. I refuse to call it untimely, because I believe God determines what is timely and what isn't. We said that in a written statement read by our pastor at his funeral, and I still believe it. God took Tom for a reason; God left us behind for a reason. The why of all of that I leave to him who made plans "for our own good" long before we were born.

God also gave us six other wonderful children to console and comfort us, as we do the same, I hope, for them.

I wish you luck with your book. I pray it will be an an instrument of healing. Thank you for asking me to participate.

In His Name,
An Anonymous Griever

The Killer AIDS

Dear Reader,

My brother died six months ago. Our family, and even a number of doctors, cannot say exactly what caused Kyle's death. Was it the mysterious spot on his lung? Was it severe internal bleeding? His death certificate listed a number of external ailments. The overwhelming fact remains that Kyle died of AIDS.

I am still working through my grief. Sometimes I cry because I miss him so much, and other times I find myself thinking of something to send him or to do during his next visit. I feel foolish when I accidently speak of him in the present tense. I loved Kyle deeply.

I remember joking about AIDS with friends at work several years earlier. Our boss interrupted our laughter. "You wouldn't joke about AIDS if you knew someone who had it." I was shocked when she didn't laugh at our word plays on *AIDS*, since she was usually the ringleader of tasteless jokes. I dismissed her comments as liberal sympathy for homosexuals who deserved the disease.

A few months later, I heard a talk show on a Christian radio station. The panel consisted mostly of people with HIV or in varying stages of the disease. I was overwhelmed as I heard accounts of their physical pain as well as emotional pain from rejection. The minister who moderated the group concluded the interview by stating that as a church, and more specifically as individual Christians, we needed to be ready to respond to the AIDS crisis before an individual situation forces us into action. He cautioned against waiting for a situation to arise. Spontaneous decisions are difficult, because a response to AIDS becomes clouded with a focus on homosexual sin, discomfort, and fear for one's own health. After the program finished, I remember praying that if God could use me, I wanted to be an example of God's forgiveness and acceptance. I wanted to be the practical extension of God's love.

I started reading information about the disease, unaware of what my commitment might involve. A few months after we moved to the San Francisco Bay area, we expected a visit from my oldest brother. Since he was sixteen years older than me, I was looking forward to his visit. I felt I really hadn't even started to know him until my college days, when I was surprised to find how many things we had in common. He appreciated the arts and music, liked traveling and enjoyed learning. A student leader and valedictorian of his senior class, Kyle had always been smart, popular, and successful.

I was disappointed when he couldn't come. I can still recall his words when he explained why. "I really am sick," he said. "I have AIDS. I wanted to tell you myself, but I don't know when I'll be well enough to travel." I was engulfed with emotion. I had to deal with the double shock that Kyle was going to die and that he had secretly led a gay lifestyle. In church that evening, while tears flooded down my cheeks, our senior pastor asked if anyone had a prayer request. I sat shaking my head no, because I wasn't ready to share this with anyone yet.

Kyle discovered he had HIV five years earlier while he was living in Hawaii. He moved back to the mainland planning to break the news of his illness as well as of his lifestyle.

At first his health was so good that it was easy to put things off. Then our family had some other crisis situations. Kyle was concerned about our parents and didn't want to add to their burden. He became weaker but tried to "keep up appearances." Before long it was Thanksgiving, then Christmas, then our parents' anniversary. Kyle didn't want to ruin special family times. Finally, after he was hospitalized with pneumonia, he knew he had to tell each of us before we figured it out on our own.

Kyle had lived in his own secret prison for several years. A banker with an MBA who had served in Vietnam—Kyle had kept his secret well. He did not expect pity. He was very aware of our family's feelings. He encouraged each of us to get support and was open to our questions. He even recommended the excellent book *How Will I Tell My Mother?* by Steve and Jerry Arterburn to prepare us for what might be ahead and to give us insight into his past life.

Kyle spent a great deal of time talking with me. Though he had accepted Christ in grade school, he had made some poor choices. He explained, "Everyone in my family and even other places said that they loved me, but I always felt that they only loved who they thought I was. I had a big dark secret, and I believed if people knew who I really was, I would be rejected." His fear of rejection was so great that he planned to commit suicide if our parents rejected him after he told them the truth. He knew that homosexuality was in direct opposition to our parents' Christian beliefs, and he'd known a number of friends who were isolated as they lay dying with AIDS. He couldn't face the possibility of rejection in addition to his suffering. Our parents' tearful, enveloping embrace shocked him and marked the beginning of reconciliation in his life.

Our family increased phone calls and visits to Kyle. He tried to see my parents at least once a week while he was still able to drive. The weekly trip guaranteed him nourishing meals and often clean laundry, car repairs, or other helps. Kyle had been very independent, so it was difficult to know how to help him. When my husband and I were able to visit, we tried to make a point of staying at his house so we could do grocery shopping, household repairs, car maintenance, cleaning, and other tasks. The rest of the family was within driving distance, so they made "drop-in" visits whenever possible. Though I struggled with being so far from Kyle, I enjoyed the visits. My husband, Scott, took extra time off to support me and encouraged me to fly back as often as possible. Though we wanted to be available to do things for Kyle, we also wanted simply to be available. For years Kyle kept his lifestyle to himself out of fear of rejection. We wanted to communicate love and acceptance to him.

We took advantage of his clinic days to escort him, meet his doctors and other caregivers, and to learn more about AIDS. The Center for Human Caring was exactly that. In a facility separate from the hospital, outpatient treatment was given. Though it had predominantly male patients, occasionally a woman or an infant came as well. It was interesting to watch while an infected homosexual man gave a young mother a break. As he held her baby, she asked how he was doing. There was no suggestion that her baby had been infected by a "homosexual disease." They both were hurting.

The staff at the Center for Human Caring was warm and creative. They solicited unusual donations to make things warm and comfortable. One time when I was visiting Kyle, the center received a number of flowers from a grocery floral department. Everyone helped sort out the fading ones. A volunteer made a special bouquet to take to a patient in the hospital who hadn't had visitors. In another room they had a piano. Some of the staff and outpatients were planning the next video party. Every Friday they scheduled appointments before noon and had a potluck lunch. The environment was very positive while it was also honest about the killer disease the patients shared. During one treatment Kyle needed to be alone. A doctor approached my husband

and me and asked how we were doing. He proceeded to answer any questions we had.

The center was a source of support for Kyle. Kyle also tried to participate in an AIDS support group, but the constant death of members and addition of new ones made trust relationships difficult. Kyle certainly didn't avoid facing death. That was impossible. During an especially low point while Kyle was hospitalized, a visitor came. Michael was tan, attractive, and carried his tennis racquet over his shoulder. A month later, Kyle was out of the hospital and doing well when he received word of Michael's death. Our family worked at finding ways to support Kyle emotionally as well as physically in ways that the support group could not offer.

We found that communication was most open when Kyle was with just one other person. During one stay at our house, Kyle and I started talking, and I completely missed Sunday school. (As a minister's wife, I usually don't do that.) I was grateful for a husband and a church that was encouraging and understanding when I chose to be with Kyle.

People sent notes and constant reminders of God's love. Friends prayed for Kyle regularly and often asked about his health. Even so, I was selective about whom I told at first. Though no one ever responded critically, I found it difficult to bring up the subject of AIDS. People sometimes make jokes about homosexuals and even AIDS victims. Therefore, my former employer in Chicago had said, "You wouldn't joke about AIDS if you knew someone who had it." I was overly sensitive at times. I wasn't always sure whom I should trust. I also tried to keep others from feeling uncomfortable. People don't expect to hear that someone has AIDS.

After a rather emotional church service, I slipped out the side door to try to regain my composure. A caring friend noticed me and came to share my tears. I had mentioned that my brother was sick and I had a hard time being one thousand miles away. She patted me compassionately and said, "Yes, it's hard to be so far away from loved ones." Through my tears and sniffles, I finally whispered that he had AIDS. Her shock was obvious. "Oh, my goodness," she said. "He really is sick." Eventually I learned that shock did not mean a person was being judgmental.

Though each member of our family found support from different sources, it was probably most difficult for my parents. They were afraid to tell many of their church friends for fear that they would be judged for accepting him or even more so for being "bad parents" who caused him to be gay. Their own minister, however, eventually figured out the situation and called them. He and another church leader were very supportive. A former pastor our family had known for years was another source of encouragement for them as well as our entire family. Interestingly, the most important support person for them was Kyle, as he communicated that they truly were good parents.

Last summer Kyle was accepted into an experimental medication program in San Francisco and lived with me for four months. As my husband and I watched him suffer and become weaker, struggle with energy and pain, we hurt for him. One time, as he lay exhausted in bed with his IV tube hanging from his chest, he said, "I would never wish this disease on my worst enemy, but if I hadn't contracted it, I would never have found reconciliation with God and with my parents." It took that kind of crisis to bring him back into fellowship with God and his family. Not that Kyle was openly rebellious, but he had a "secret" that isolated him.

I was reminded that God sees the big picture and is able, through his providence, to work things for our greatest good, even though we may not know how. Sometimes I become frustrated with God for choosing to end Kyle's life so early. And if he did have to, why couldn't he have had a brain tumor or cancer or something that wouldn't make me so uncomfortable when I tell others? However, now I realize that God would not have accomplished his plan that way. Even though Kyle was suffering, in hindsight he would not have chosen different circumstances. Kyle even said that he'd never felt so genuinely loved as when people knew everything about him and chose to love him anyway.

While Kyle was with us, I was touched by the response of a number of people in our church. Some of the members I might have categorized as the most offended by Kyle's former gay lifestyle were the most gracious in terms of reaching out to him. He kept saying, "I can't believe people are so nice to me."

People often gave of themselves in ways that were uniquely their own. A family offered to stay with Kyle when we had to be out of town for the weekend. (I didn't even have to ask anyone!) A mother of three boys brought homemade chocolate chip cookies and stayed to visit. (The cookies were a great treat during hours of IV infusions!) A teenager from our church brought newspapers to read. Our friends Rick and Joni came to visit us from out of state. Joni and I sat on Kyle's bed and prayed for him while he had a 104° fever. When Kyle and I were alone together, he asked, "Do they know what's wrong with me? Do they realize how I got AIDS? Aren't they afraid of me?" He wasn't used to Christians who were so loving. He knew God's forgiveness, but man's forgiveness was not always predictable. Later Rick and Joni were playing the piano and singing. Kyle made the difficult trip downstairs to hear them better. Though there wasn't much anyone could do to comfort him physically, he found joy in their music.

In August of last summer his condition worsened and he needed to make an emergency trip back to his home doctor. We tried desperately to arrange a flight but couldn't because of complications. Without even being asked, a travel agent in our church went to work on the situation. He not only got a flight for Kyle that day but also arranged skycap service and had a cab waiting in Denver. He even offered his comfortable van and drove us to the airport so Scott and I wouldn't have to hassle the traffic. The travel agent didn't know a lot about AIDS, but he knew about airports and made himself available.

People also made themselves available to Scott and me as well. One evening as Kyle was resting, and Scott was out of town, a friend showed up at my door with a two-for-one yogurt coupon. She promised we'd only take twenty minutes. I didn't realize how much I needed to get out! People found creative ways to give support.

I was grateful for the quantity of time to spend with Kyle that summer. Because we lived so far away, I had often felt there was little I could do. At our house I could fix meals, do laundry, and take care of some of his needs. Though Kyle had little energy, we tried to take scenic drives on Scott's days off. Occasionally, we'd even go out for a special dinner.

Though the outpatient clinic days in San Francisco were not as positive as our times had been at the Center for Human Caring, we tried to find things to do. Between appointments we'd enjoy a cookie in the cafeteria that overlooked the ocean. Other times we'd stop for coffee on the way home. When Kyle had to be in the hospital, my husband initiated a two-hour pass for him to go out for lunch and watch the seals before his next treatment. Another time we picked up a pizza and brought it to his hospital room. Garden flowers, peanuts, magazines, and juice boxes were also easy to deliver. Since his diet was not restricted, he always enjoyed a change from hospital food.

The time at our house was also a time for Kyle to make funeral plans. He and Scott got along well and talked openly. Kyle wanted Scott to do the service. Kyle wanted it to be upbeat and hopeful. They talked about different ideas. Kyle wrote down song choices such as "Great Is Thy Faithfulness," "It Is Well With My Soul," "Joyful, Joyful, We Adore Thee," and "There is Joy in the Journey." Though he only expected five or six friends in addition to the family, he wanted to communicate the hope and forgiveness he knew.

After he made the emergency trip to his hometown, he spent several weeks in the hospital. Pneumonia and infection because of the IV tube in his chest weakened him even more. When he was released, he continued to make arrangements for his death. He finalized his will and made sure all of his accounts were in order and papers were organized. He made plans with a funeral home and consulted family members about their personal wishes. He was very thorough. He didn't want to be a burden.

Our family was all together for Thanksgiving. Kyle and Scott discussed more of the arrangements for the service. Kyle made a list of people who should be notified after his death. Each time we left we wondered if it would be our last time to see him. It was hard to say good-bye. One time Kyle scolded me and told me not to cry when he died. I joked back, "I cried when you moved to Hawaii and I'll cry when you move to heaven. I know you'll be in a wonderful place, but I'm not sure when I'll see you again! I'll miss you."

Kyle's condition continued to deteriorate. Because he preferred to stay at home, my parents visited each week to stay with him, take him to the hospital, and do all they could. In January he was admitted to the hospital again. While in the hospital, one doctor asked Kyle why he was continuing to hang on and suffer. He asked if there was anyone he needed to ask permission to die. Later Kyle asked my parents if they were willing to let him go.

As time went on, Kyle's condition seemed to improve. My parents returned to their own home on Thursday expecting Kyle to be released from the hospital the following Monday.

On Friday, Kyle's abdominal pain became more severe; he asked a visiting friend to call Mom and Dad from the hospital. When they arrived, he asked them to pray that God would take him. Confident in his hope of eternal life, my parents prayed out loud that God would graciously take him from his suffering. Within a few minutes he died in Mom's and Dad's arms. He died knowing he was loved and accepted rather than rejected and isolated as he once feared.

I had planned to stay home alone that evening but spontaneously changed my mind to go out with Scott. We came home and were together when my parents called to say that Kyle had died. In addition to our grief, we had to ask people to cover our responsibilities. A dear couple came at midnight to cry and pray with us. They were aware of all we had to do and didn't stay long. The love of our church family meant so much, especially with our extended family so far away.

The next several days were a blur. Our entire family stayed at Kyle's place. We grieved together, laughed together, and sometimes drove each other crazy. We shared funny memories. We shared regrets. I had planned to visit Kyle the following weekend.

There was a blizzard on the night of Kyle's funeral. Our former pastor came to sing, and Scott celebrated the freedom of forgiveness that Christ offers each of us. Over a hundred people arrived to express their sympathy. It was truly a joyous celebration of Kyle's earthly and eternal life.

Throughout his life Kyle had a compassion and concern for others. He chose to put the needs of others ahead of his own, even when he was ill. He never wanted to put anyone out of their way on his account, even though he had helped many others.

We cried and hugged Kyle's friends we recognized from hospital visits and others we'd never met. One woman came whose son had died of AIDS a few months before. A young man came. The next day we discovered he also had AIDS. He had heard about Kyle's condition and wanted to share his own testimony, if Kyle wasn't a Christian. The son of a Baptist minister, he had become involved in a homosexual lifestyle. Now he sees AIDS as the escape God provided to bring him back into fellowship. My parents continue to keep in touch with him.

Recently, my parents came to California to visit. We are close, and it was a special time to be together. We looked through sympathy cards and talked about Kyle. They seemed especially grateful to visit the hospital where Kyle had been. At our church they met people who had reached out to Kyle while he was with us. They felt love and support from people they barely knew. We also spent time just having fun together. It had been an especially intense couple of years for my parents, and they deserved a real vacation.

While driving by the coast one afternoon, I mentioned that Kyle especially enjoyed that view as well as Golden Gate Park nearby. My father said, "He always enjoyed beautiful scenery. I guess he's surrounded by the best now."

At my parents' request I have changed some of the names in Kyle's story. Unfortunately, there are still many people whose response to AIDS is far from compassionate. I'm reminded of Ryan White's grave being continually vandalized. I have purposely tried to protect our family's anonymity. However, I often wish I could have named my parents—not to betray them, but to honor them. They are the "heroes" of this story. Though many people touched Kyle's life, their love and acceptance outweighed all the others'.

Recently a Christian friend told me how proud she was that her sister had the courage to kick her homosexual son out of the house and let him know that he was not welcome back as long as he had "that sin" in his life. My heart broke. How sad it is that we, who have been so freely forgiven, often reject others who are hurting.

I have the utmost respect for my parents' response to Kyle.

> In His love,
> A Grieving Sister

To summarize this chapter I offer helpers the following reminders.

1. Our calling is to unconditionally accept and love the dying person and the family regardless of circumstances. We should avoid the trap of analyzing

why this happened or suggesting the blame of family members. Judgment has no place here.

2. A profound result of AIDS, which often is an outcome of a "deep, dark secret" that has tormented for years, is that it forces a family to have no more secrets. Open, honest sharing, perhaps done for the first time, becomes the family's way of dealing with the illness and death. God's purpose is healing—the perfect example of "Satan meant it for evil but God meant it for good."

3. Kyle's sister told me that God did not heal Kyle, but he did walk the road with him, miraculously working out every detail. God did this through people—people who brought cookies, made travel arrangements, wrote letters, prayed, sang songs, did household tasks, and more. It struck me that each person probably thought that he or she did little, that their task was insignificant. Yet through all these individual servants, God did much. Helpers must realize that God works out his plan through the little things. All are his available hands for the detail work and the helpers' job is to be alert for those opportunities. A loving, supportive church family is God's greatest tool.

4. Note the support chain that Kyle's story shows us. Kyle's sister and parents helped him as he died. Kyle helped them say good-bye and prepare for his death. After Kyle was gone, his sister continued to help her parents grieve, sharing their pain. Helpers are no substitutes for effective families. The helper's role is to encourage family members to share honestly and help each other grieve.

13

A Family Portrait

I recently met a young woman, Diana, who told me about her sister who died when Diana was eight years old. I asked her if she would write her story to tell helpers what a sibling experiences. She graciously agreed to do so. Her mother and father were also willing to contribute their stories.

This "family portrait" is a powerful illustration of the principles covered in this book, and a fitting conclusion. Note how the church both helped and did not help them. Note how the medical staff both supported them and did not support them. Observe what brought them comfort and what caused pain. View their different perspectives of the same experience. Think about how you would have helped them.

A Mother's Grief

The colors of the leaves were especially bright for our family that fall of 1970. We were finally settled into a small community on San Francisco Bay. Living in a rented house, we had purchased a lot, and our thoughts were occupied with the home we would soon build. Our family consisted of my husband, Don, and our daughters Donna, six, and Diana, five.

Don worked for a large utility company, and I had signed a contract to teach a first grade class in a local school. We were active in our local church—Don in music and church leadership, I teaching Sunday school, and together leading a youth group that met on Wednesday evenings (and any other time they could think of an excuse to get together). Our life was full.

The bliss was short lived, however. The second day after school started, Diana, out playing with a friend, pulled an old-fashioned wagon wheel across her foot. The result was many stitches, a broken toe, and eventual plastic surgery on her foot.

Halloween came, and the girls' entry into the local children's parade required some extra ingenuity since Diana's foot was still in a cast. The consensus was that they would dress as clowns, we would decorate their wagon, and Donna would pull the wagon with Diana in it. They looked festive as they started down the street.

In the second block of the parade, Donna looked at her dad and said, "I need help. I can't pull this wagon." So her dad pulled the wagon. Donna had expressed tiredness other times that fall, and I had dismissed them to the fact that we weren't quite used to the routine of school. Our district was on half-day sessions that year. I taught a morning session, and the girls attended the afternoon session. Since this necessitated dropping them off for child care by 7:15 each morning, I wasn't surprised to hear complaints of "I'm tired."

Not long after Halloween, the entire family was stricken with stomach flu. While Don, Diana, and I recovered rapidly, Donna did not. Her fever remained high, and she was lethargic. The doctor administered one form of antibiotic followed by a second, more potent one. When there was no response to either drug, Donna was hospitalized. The doctor told me he suspected pneumonia.

Donna was given a private room, and the hospital allowed me to stay in the room with her. After the X rays showed nothing, the doctor began looking further.

The *Readers' Digest* of November 1970 carried an article about St. Jude's Hospital and the work being done there on leukemia. Having read that and observing the doctor's glum countenance, I found myself blurting out the question, "Is there any chance this could be leukemia?" He responded in the affirmative, and thus began a new page in our life's story.

I remember reading Romans, chapter 8, during those days, trying to understand the events that were taking place. There was too much to try to understand, and so I feebly did the best I could to give it to God and rely on the prayers and comfort of the many friends who rallied around at that time.

Our general practitioner called in a hematologist. A bone marrow aspiration for biopsy was attempted, the needle broke, another needle was unavailable, so the procedure had to be done again the next day. The second attempt was successful, and before I knew it, the doctor was sitting in Donna's hospital room, arms folded across his chest, and "It's confirmed" spilling out of his mouth.

I was numb. I followed him out the door and asked him what we could expect. His reply included the possibility of chemotherapy at a nearby university hospital. I asked him about time. He shrugged his shoulders and without a change in his expression said, "Two to four weeks, two to four months, who knows?" I couldn't believe the callousness in his voice. Finally I asked him if he had children of his own, and, his voice softening, he said, "Three."

I said, "Then maybe you can understand what we're going through." With that, he walked away.

The next day was Donna's seventh birthday, and since the doctor was sure it would be her last birthday, he signed orders that anyone who wanted to come could be in her room. My mother had come to take care of Diana while we were at the hospital, and I remember crying on the trip to the bakery with her to pick up Donna's "last" birthday cake. Our friends and loved ones came, we all put on very brave masks, and we "celebrated" Donna's birthday.

Not knowing where to turn for advice, but feeling there had to be better treatment options than the one offered, Don called the American Cancer Society. His call was returned two days later by an empathetic listener who said that if the child were his daughter or granddaughter, he would take her to M. D. Anderson Hospital and Tumor Institute, operated by the University of Texas in Houston. We discussed this information with our admitting doctor, and he made a phone call to Houston. The next day Don, Donna, and I were on a plane bound for Houston. My mother packed my suitcase; I didn't even go home. As we left the hospital in the early morning hours, the nurses cried with me.

During the time Donna was in the hospital, Diana had been released by the plastic surgeon. My mother brought her to the hospital to share the good news and show off the new shoes that now fit both feet. It was a relief to have my mother there caring for Diana and helping Don manage things at home. As we left for Houston, plans were made for my mother to take Diana to southern California to stay with my brother and sister-in-law until we returned.

Few people realize how a child's terminal illness affects the entire family. My mother had intestinal problems for a year. I grieved for Donna. Mother grieved for Donna and me (her child).

Our arrival at M. D. Anderson brought both relief and anxiety: relief at being in a pediatric oncology unit where my child was not the sickest one and anxiety over what was to come. We were soon initiated into the traumas of bone marrow aspirations, chemotherapy, IVs that infiltrate, and the raging appetite that seems to accompany large doses of prednisone.

We were touched deeply by the outpouring of concern by the people of Houston. We had arrived on Saturday, and late that afternoon someone came to ask if we would be interested in attending church services the next morning in the hospital chapel. When we responded in the affirmative, we were told that someone would be in Donna's room to escort us to the chapel, since we were unfamiliar with the hospital. And so, even though we were deep into our own thoughts and confusion, it was good to be worshiping with others in a similar situation that Sunday morning. Sunday school classes for the patients were held on Sunday afternoons. Nearby churches rotated the responsibility of conducting the sessions. Each time Donna attended Sunday school, she returned to her room with a tangible reminder of the day's lesson, which served as an encouragement to me, too.

In addition to church services, the children were frequently entertained by puppet troupes, handbell choirs, and even the Texas Rangerettes. Even very ill children were wheeled to the playroom in wheelchairs or on gurneys to enjoy the entertainment.

It was interesting to observe, however, the stoicism on the faces of the young patients during even the funniest entertainment. After an excellent performance by a group of teenage puppeteers, I overheard one of them comment that the children didn't appear to enjoy it. I explained to the performer that, even though the children did not appear to enjoy the show, they would be talking about it long after the troupe had left.

It was a phenomenon I observed several times during Donna's hospitalizations: Children in a hospital setting, in various phases of treatment and illness, did not seem to respond as spontaneously to live entertainment

144

as they would have outside the hospital environment. My hope is that anyone generous enough with his time or talents to be willing to go to a hospital to entertain children with life-threatening illnesses would not be discouraged by their seeming lack of response.

Thanksgiving was in the week following our arrival in Houston. I remember feeling isolated, missing Diana, being two thousand miles away from the traditional family get-together, so unsure of what the future would hold. While I was able to give thanks for being in a place that offered hope for Donna through an aggressive treatment protocol, it was difficult to give thanks for everything as we are reminded to do in Ephesians 5:20.

Don left for home the Sunday following Thanksgiving. I felt alone and on my own after he left. The phone calls, letters, and packages from California were constant reminders that we were in the thoughts and prayers of those who loved us, and they sustained Donna and me as our daily routine centered around blood counts, temperature readings, and watching the IV bottle to be sure it didn't run dry.

Don's home stay was short, however. After a week Donna's temperature rose to a frightening 106°, her counts were low, and the doctor suggested calling her father to return, since Donna's condition was so unstable. Our reserve funds were depleted, and we began learning the lessons of grace and humility as we gratefully accepted money that had been raised by our youth group, as well as donations from complete strangers, to pay for Don's return trip to Houston. While Don had a good job, he had used all his available vacation time on the first trip and so was taking personal leave to return to Houston. He remained in Houston until Donna was "out of the woods" and left with the knowledge that soon our family would be reunited, hopefully for Christmas.

As Don left for the second time, my mother came to be with us. We were fortunate to have been granted the use of a small cottage maintained by a local Houston church for the sole purpose of providing housing for families of pediatric oncology patients at M. D. Anderson (an early version of the Ronald McDonald House). Donna's health gradually improved, we were granted outpatient status, and on December 23 we boarded a plane for Los Angeles to spend Christmas with Diana and the rest of our family.

We celebrated a glorious Christmas! It didn't matter that I had done no Christmas shopping or any of the usual holiday preparations. All that mattered was that we were together.

Our tranquility was brief, however. Don had driven to southern California, and on December 26 we left for home, bound to keep an appointment with a pediatric oncologist at Children's Hospital in Oakland on December 27. Donna and I went to Oakland expecting a routine checkup; the next thing we knew, she was admitted for a new course of chemotherapy. It was disappointing, since we had so much looked forward to being reunited as a family and home for the first time in nearly two months.

The biggest disappointment was being in the hospital on December 30, when Diana celebrated her sixth birthday. A vivid picture that jumps off the page of the photo album each time I come across it is of Diana passing out candy to the members of the youth group that evening. She appears to be trying to snuggle up to one of the teenagers while being ignored. I think it depicts some of the struggles she faced during her sister's illness. Donna was released the next day, and we were finally home.

During Donna's stay at Children's Hospital at Oakland, it became apparent that I was going to be unable to cope with her regimen of chemotherapy, fluctuating blood counts, and with first graders learning to read, all at the same time. I approached the principal of my school with a request for a leave of absence for the remainder of the school year. However, since this was just my second year with the district, and they had over-hired for the year, the district insisted on a resignation. The teachers' union approached me about fighting for the leave of absence, but I simply had no energy with which to fight. So, reluctantly I resigned my teaching position.

For the next two courses of chemotherapy Donna's medications were started in Oakland and then given to her by a local physician who agreed to administer them. For the late-night dose we would call the doctor at his home, bundle Donna into the car, and by the time we got there, he would have the medication mixed and ready to inject. After following this regimen for three months, Donna and I went to Children's Hospital at Oakland, stayed in the doctors' dormitory, and checked into the emergency room every six hours for her chemotherapy. During this time I was being trained to mix her medications and inject them through the heparin-lock needle implanted in her vein.

Discipline can become difficult with a terminally ill child. On the one hand is the heavy sense of not wanting to inflict any more upon the child. However, after being around rude, unruly children at the clinic whose parents seemed to avoid any type of discipline, we decided we would not tolerate that kind of behavior. While Donna was not a difficult child, she would sometimes push us on certain issues.

One night at the dinner table, while she was undergoing chemotherapy, was one of those times. Don told her that if she didn't obey, he would have to spank her. She looked at him in surprise and asked, "With my needle in?" He replied, "Yes, with your needle in."

She said, "Oh!"

That was the end of the discussion and the end of the problem. Somehow she needed to know that our demands on her behavior had not changed.

Donna loved school and was an avid reader. When we took her to the ophthalmologist to correct a vision problem, he actually said, "Why waste your money on getting her glasses? She will die soon anyway." How could a doctor—a "healer"—be so cruel?

The next few months were relatively calm. I taught a half-day kindergarten class in a new Christian school. Donna was in second grade and Diana in first. I did learn one important lesson during that time, however.

We had been invited to a wedding in a small town in Arizona. The way I figured it, we would camp at the north rim of the Grand Canyon for a week, go to the wedding, and then be home in time for the next round of chemotherapy. We went to the doctor for what I thought would be a routine checkup and blood count. After examining her, the doctor told Donna he was going to do a bone marrow biopsy and start her chemotherapy, which would cut into our camping trip. I fell apart. The nurses got a social worker to calm the crying mother and assure me that things would work out.

And they did. We went to the wedding and then went camping at the north rim. We were concerned about recovering blood counts, but had a wonderful vacation, nevertheless. From that time on, I learned more about living one day at a time, that it's okay to make plans, and to realize that they might change due to unforeseen circumstances.

School began in 1972 without incident. However, as September turned into October, Donna would occasionally complain of headaches. She seemed to become more lethargic, although according to the doctor, there was no medical reason for it.

I wondered if she might be depressed. Her ninth birthday was coming soon, so we planned a birthday party, hoping it would cheer her up. The guests came, and as we were playing games, she became ill and spent the rest of the party sick. Still no clues, the doctor said.

We decided to go to southern California, hoping the change of scenery might help. Donna spent most of the time lying on the couch instead of playing with her cousins. My sister-in-law arranged for a horse (Donna's favorite animal) to be brought to the house for rides. Donna couldn't even get off the couch to pet the horse.

My heart was heavy as we headed for home and a Monday appointment with the doctor. After examining her, he told us he must perform a spinal tap. We knew the possibility of the disease showing up in the central nervous system, and in those days children did not long survive once that happened.

Don and I were in the room when the doctor performed the spinal tap, and we understood the significance of the moment when the fluid went to the top of the gauge. The doctor walked with us to the parking lot that afternoon and cried with us. The chemotherapy introduced into her spinal column that day brought a welcome relief from the headaches and the added trauma of regular spinal taps.

Early 1973 found us making daily trips to Oakland for spinal/cranial radiation. Donna lost her hair, so we purchased two wigs: one that closely matched her hair color and style, and a blond, curly wig for fun. On windy days when I picked her up at school, she would be the only child on the playground with her coat on and the hood tied down tight.

We visited her aunt and uncle shortly after Donna lost all her hair. She decided to wear the natural-looking wig, since my sister-in-law had not told our two nephews that Donna was bald.

The children, who were fairly close in age, always seemed to pick up their play where they had left off the visit before. They hadn't been playing long on this visit when Donna asked, "Is it okay if I take it off?" I said it was up to her, so she grabbed her wig and said, "Here, Rob, catch!" One can only imagine the expression on her cousins' faces as they faced this bald girl. Then they all started to laugh.

We got the blonde wig from the car, the kids all got out their sunglasses, and we have irreplaceable pictures of the four of them having a great time. My sister-in-law had been telling my oldest nephew that if he didn't quit wearing his favorite greasy hat, all his hair would fall out. She didn't have to remind him again after our visit!

One fond memory of Children's Hospital at Oakland was the Christmas party for the oncology patients. The children's doctor dressed up as Santa Claus, his nurse as Santa's elf, and entire families joined the festivities held in the doctors' lounge. The gifts the children received were brought by the parents but handed out by Santa in a grand manner.

In the spring of 1973 Donna's doctor joined the staff at Stanford. We were given the opportunity to transfer to Stanford, and we opted to go. The facility there was airy, the rooms large and modern in contrast to Oakland's old hospital, and it was good to see familiar faces on the medical team. We were even able to eat meals family-style together in the dining room.

It soon seemed the car could make the seventy-mile, one-way trip to Stanford by itself. Several times that spring I would take Donna down there after teaching my morning class of kindergartners, expecting to be home by early evening, only to find out she needed a blood transfusion. By the time a type and cross-match was done and the blood infused, it would be ten or eleven o'clock at night. The more frequently this occurred, the more I had to rely on good friends for Diana's care.

I have always been thankful that Diana seemed to have been born independent. Before she learned to walk, I would sometimes miss her only to find her in her bedroom playing by herself. I believe it was this characteristic that allowed her to be flexible about who picked her up from school on days when I was detained in Palo Alto. We were blessed with some special friends who always opened their home to Donna when her counts were too low for her to go to school, and to Diana when I couldn't be there for her after school.

Another blessing at that time was a wonderful housekeeper who came in once a week and did everything—changed the beds, did all the laundry, the ironing, and cleaned the house. She did this for us even if we weren't there to give her a check that day. As I look back, she played a major part in our day-to-day survival.

Donna's hair was beginning to grow back, and it came in curly. The first time she ventured out without her wig was to walk two blocks to a neighborhood store to buy some vanilla for a baking project. She was dressed in a brightly colored pants outfit and came home fighting mad. The clerk in the store had asked, "May I help you, son?"

I asked her how she replied, and she said, "I asked where the vanilla was."

Another time she and her dad were in a restaurant, and the waitress asked what she could bring "you gentlemen."

Her dad gave his order and then said, "And she'll have. . . ." We laughed about it, and so did Donna.

Donna's blood counts were too low to allow her to use public facilities of any kind in the summer of 1972, so we borrowed my parents' travel trailer and enjoyed a delightful week camping at the edge of the Smith River in the redwoods.

The fall of 1972 found Donna admitted for a relapse. Her system managed to recover; however, Donna's health seemed more fragile. My memory is a blur of short hospital stays relieved by times of relative calm. Christmas that year was a warm family get-together at my sister and brother-in-law's. Everyone seemed to have a sense that it might be Donna's last Christmas; and while we tried hard not to overindulge her, her Christmas wish list was fulfilled.

Children's Hospital at Stanford became our home for all but eight weeks of eight months in 1973. The relapses came more frequently, and the recovery from chemotherapy took longer. Diana spent two weeks in southern California with my parents in February that year, and at the ripe old age of eight, flew home alone at the end of her stay.

As Palm Sunday, 1973, dawned, Donna ran a high fever, and once again we were on our way to Stanford. It had become evident that we had to find a semipermanent place for Diana, since she had stayed with first one friend and then another. That Sunday morning I packed her things, sadly called my sister, and asked her to come to take Diana to live with her. It was a difficult decision, because I knew I would not see Diana often from that distance, yet I knew she needed to be in one place with people who loved her and could provide a consistent routine. After Easter vacation my sister enrolled Diana for the last quarter of second grade in a school where I had not even met the teacher. It was both a relief and a heartache to have her there.

Don worked closer to Stanford than he did to home, so we made arrangements to park my parents' travel trailer on the hospital grounds, and he stayed there most of the time. It also became a wonderful "retreat" for Donna. She found the bathtub fit her just right, and she enjoyed a leisurely bath out there several times. Sometimes we spent the night out there, and when the nurse would knock on the door reminding us that the doctors were making rounds and that we should go back into her hospital room, Donna would roll her eyes as if to say, "Get lost!"

Don attempted to contact churches in the Palo Alto area regarding a Sunday school program or church services similar to those at M. D. Anderson in Houston, only to find there was very little interest in that type of ministry at that time. It was discouraging.

A school was adjacent to the hospital, and those children who were able were expected to attend regularly. The teacher was a warm, sensitive person. Donna looked forward to attending, and I enjoyed the brief respites.

A Fourth of July barbecue was planned at the hospital by the parents of the oncology patients. One of the doctors volunteered to be the head chef. Delicious steaks were donated, and even though the hospital food was palatable, this potluck affair was a real treat. That evening about dusk the medical personnel left, and the children were treated to a fireworks display put on by the parents. We found out later that Palo Alto had a law restricting the use of fireworks, and the hospital was cited the next day. In the meantime, the children were delighted!

During Donna's illness, we tried to "seize the moment" whenever time, her health, and resources permitted. As spring droned into the summer of 1973, she suffered several setbacks. We tried to get away from the hospital as often as possible on short-term passes. I remember one summery day when she stood looking out the window and sighed, "This is no way to spend a summer." My heart ached for her and for the time so long before, it seemed, when she would spend her summer days playing outside all day.

Donna enjoyed fishing and began talking about how she would like to go fishing. So on a Sunday afternoon, just two weeks before she died and while she was confined to a wheelchair with leukemic arthritis, we bundled her up and took her to a trout farm to fish. Diana was visiting that weekend (staying with Don in the travel trailer), so she was able to join the excursion. The fish were biting, and the girls were having a great time, but soon we had to tell Diana to stop fishing so we could afford to pay for all the fish they caught!

Donna's condition continued to deteriorate, and one August day she went into congestive heart failure. The doctors offered the possibilities of some extraordinary procedures in an attempt to prolong her life. It seemed, however, that it was time to let her go. She had fought gallantly, and through our tears we had watched her suffer. On the afternoon of August 11, with her dad and me at her side, she slipped from this life into the arms of Jesus.

As evidence of God's supreme care for us, the pastor/administrator of the Christian school where I taught walked into the hospital room about the time Donna died and was there to offer comfort and support. At the moment of her death, I remember feeling as though an enormous load had been lifted. No longer would there be needles, bone marrow biopsies, blood transfusions, and the various other tests and procedures that had dominated our lives for the last thirty-three months.

Three days later a simple graveside service was held for family and close friends. A week after her death a memorial service to celebrate her life, rather than mourn her death, took place in our local church. A lovely meal was hosted by the women of the church following the service, and because we were exhausted and numb, their efforts meant much.

Having been in the hospital for such a long time, we developed friendships with the parents of other patients. A loosely organized network was established with people across the country who had come to Stanford for treatment. And so it was, following Donna's memorial service, that Don, Diana, and I boarded a plane for Orlando, Florida, to spend a week with a family whose oldest son had died in June. Our pastor had encouraged us to make the trip, and we were grateful to him for his advice. It was a time of rest and reflection before we rejoined the "real world" of regular trips to the supermarket, gas lines (1974), work, school, meals at our kitchen table, and dirty dishes.

Pediatric oncology nurses have to be one step closer to sainthood than the rest of us! Their job is one of the most demanding and emotionally draining I have ever observed. Their keeping the IVs running reminded me of entertainers who twirl plates on sticks and try to keep all the plates going without letting them crash to the floor and break. Additionally, they must be patient with distraught parents and patients undergoing trauma.

The head of the pediatric oncology unit at M. D. Anderson, and subsequently at Children's Hospital at Stanford, was a man who believed strongly that parents should play an active role in their child's care, even when the child was hospitalized. To that end, a cot was provided next to each child's bed so that one parent could spend the night with the child. Later, when we met with parents of other children with cancer who were being treated in facilities with different philosophies regarding parents' participation in the care of their children and which required the parents to observe the hospital visiting hours, I realized how fortunate we were to be treated as responsible, involved individuals, and not as mere bystanders.

This philosophy may have had its drawbacks, however. As I look at it in retrospect, Donna's illness and treatment became all-consuming to me, and I assumed it did to Don as well. I have since learned about the very different ways men and women express emotions and realize that, as I was totally immersed in Donna's care, I paid little attention to Don's emotional pain and was unable to get far enough beyond myself to attempt to meet him in his place of grief.

The head of the oncology department had weekly meetings with parents where issues were discussed and any questions could be asked. Here we were presented with discouraging statistics about the high percentages of parents of children with terminal illnesses who end up in divorce court (75 percent at the time), and the alarming percentages of siblings of children with catastrophic illnesses who have difficulties dealing with the upheaval. Today I understand the divorce rate is 90 percent.

Even though the department had the advantage of a full-time social worker, from my present perspective it seems that ongoing, regularly scheduled, personal counseling might have helped both Don and me better express our pain and communicate our deep needs. Essentially, our marriage was put on hold for nearly three years. And even though it would be much later and under circumstances that seemed far removed from Donna's illness and death that we found ourselves in the throes of a disintegrating marriage and divorce, one cannot help but wonder how deeply the personal and corporate growth of our relationship was crippled by this experience. To all appearances, we handled very well the trauma of losing our child, kept our remaining family intact, and were able to go on with life, but we also did well in masking the overpowering pain.

This seems an appropriate place to acknowledge the large amount of information regarding dependent/co-dependent relationships that was only in its formulative stages in the early seventies. I believe that had this information been available then to those who dealt with people in crisis, the outcome in our case might have been different.

Recognizing that the way we relate to others is a reflection of our life circumstances and experiences, I must comment on the local church as it related to us. Don was a deacon and minister of music. Together we were advisors to an active youth group that met twice weekly in our home, we were Sunday school teachers, and we tried to attend as many adult fellowship activities as time and energy would permit. When we returned from Houston following our initial stay at Oakland Children's Hospital, we tried to resume life as it had been before. Our church demands were no less, and even though other people were very considerate and expressed concern, we did little to allow ourselves some relief, nor were we counseled to do so by our pastor. Conversely, the thinking of those around us may have been to keep us as involved as possible so that we would not feel left out or have time to deal with the pain. Nevertheless, the demands were there, and I believe we took upon ourselves unnecessary guilt if we didn't meet those demands with smiling faces.

One incident stands out in my memory. We wanted to take a weekend trip at a time when Donna was doing well but we didn't do so because it would take us away from church on Sunday. We were reminded that our responsibilities "to God" had to come first.

I now know that God knows the pain in our hearts, and while he does not condone irresponsibility, he is not as rigid as some may portray him to be. He is an understanding God.

The support of friends and loved ones sustained us through the darkest days. On one occasion we arrived home on a weekend pass to find that some friends had chopped and cleared the weeds in our yard. The community had a blood drive that benefitted Donna. We were the recipients of innumerable acts of love and kindness that always seemed to come at the time they were most needed.

Those early months following Donna's death were not easy for me. I went back to teaching that fall, and we attempted to resume life as we had known it before. Sleeping was often fitful for me, and there were nights when I would wake up in a sheer panic because I wasn't at the hospital. A sense of guilt overwhelmed me at the thought of leaving her there alone. After two or three months, I moved her, in my dreams, to a rest home. I finally talked to my pastor about these disturbing, restless nights, and he assured me it was part of the process of letting go. Finally, after about six months, a dream envisioned Donna well and running across a grassy field chasing a kite. I finally had let her go!

The first year was the most difficult. Each holiday season and Donna's birthday brought tides of emotion that seemed unending. Don found it too painful to visit Donna's grave, so I often went alone. I will always be thankful for one particular friend who had an uncanny way of calling when I felt lowest. She always let me talk, and I usually dissolved in tears. Many times following such conversations she would be at my doorstep—just there. She didn't try to "fix" anything, or discount the pain, but she was there. She listened and let me know she cared. I was too paralyzed to ask for help. I am grateful that she took the initiative.

I have felt, through the years, a sense of inadequacy and guilt over being separated from Diana at such a formative time in her life. I pray that Diana has come to an understanding that we did the best we knew to do for her, given the choices at the time. For any neglect she may have perceived, I have asked her forgiveness. I am continually thankful that she has grown into a sensitive young woman who makes her contribution to society through her teaching profession.

Two years after Donna's death, God graciously sent us another precious baby girl. Dayna has been a blessing to our family; her arrival brought us much joy. I lived on pins and needles until Dayna reached her tenth birthday, constantly rushing her to the doctor at the first hint of any illness.

I discussed this writing project with Dayna, who is now sixteen, and asked her if she had any reflections about Donna's story. She replied that while she knows she has another sister she will see in heaven one day, she really can't relate to her at all. Dayna knows that we get sad around Donna's birthday, but she can't really share in the sadness.

How does one go on after an experience like this? In my opinion, it requires a faith in someone much greater than me, and for me that someone is Jesus Christ. He is my rock. During our long stay at Stanford I observed parents struggling in many ways to come to grips with the illness and impending death of their children. Some turned to alcohol to ease their pain, only to find nothing had changed when they awoke from their drunkenness. Some, who did not acknowledge a power greater than themselves, became angry and bitter. Others found, as I did, that having faith in God's ultimate plan for our lives was the only way we could comprehend this experience.

Eighteen years have passed since Donna's death, and yet a Christmas has not gone by when I haven't shed tears of emptiness. It usually happens in a quiet moment after we finish trimming the tree and always seems to catch me by surprise. Her birthday brings memories of joy mixed with sorrow.

I have found the grief-recovery process to be an on-going one. Just as each individual learns to walk and talk according to a built-in clock, so goes the difficult task of grieving. Yet those of us who have experienced the pain of losing one of the most precious gifts God bestows on humankind must pass through the tunnel of grief before we reach the light at the other end—resumption of a productive life. I have found it helpful to appreciate each moment without projecting into the future or dwelling too much on the past. The feeling that we did the best we knew to do for Donna medically and to support her emotionally through her challenges is comforting. By the grace of God, the comfort of his Holy

Spirit, the love and support of caring friends, and living one moment at a time, the days and years have passed. Philippians 3:13 and all of chapter 4 are comforting and challenging. Don said it often, and I have found it to be true, "It never gets easy; it becomes hard less often."

Recently I have become involved with the Make-A-Wish Foundation. This is an organization dedicated to providing the wish child and the immediate family with a respite, however brief, from the rigors of dealing with a life-threatening illness. Approximately 90 percent of all monies raised for Make-A-Wish go directly to granting wishes. Going on interviews, participating in informational workshops, and meeting with people whose philanthropic energy is dedicated to making life easier even for a moment for these brave children and their families—all have helped me complete this particular chapter in my life.

Doral Matlock
September 1991

A Sister's Grief

I lost my sister when I was eight years old. She died from leukemia at nine years of age.

My position in the family is quite unique. I have been the youngest child, an only child, am currently the oldest, and am technically the middle child. Confused? No, I wasn't—just lost.

Donna and I were always social creatures. She, of course, being older, was the leader; I padded dutifully and gullibly behind. Donna was the epitome of the tomboy, I the princess. Consequently, the kids who came over were often the rough-and-tumble kind who climbed our tree house, walked the beam which spanned the distance between the tree and the wisteria-laden trellis covering a walkway, and jumped down. Donna was willowy, I was chunky. Donna was witty, crafty, and saw through people. I trusted everyone, believed everything, and could be conned easily. We loved each other, and she watched out for me, even when I didn't want her to.

When I was in kindergarten I injured my foot and was hospitalized. When I came home, Donna was sick, presumably with the flu. I remember her lying listlessly on the couch watching television. Eventually my parents took her to the hospital as well, and like me, she didn't come home right away. Her stay, however, was not a fix-it ordeal like mine. Eventually I became familiar with such words as *pneumonia, leukemia, IV, chemotherapy*, and a myriad of other medical terms—words none of my other kindergarten friends had ever heard.

I was not at the hospital when the doctor told my parents what was wrong with Donna's body, but I recreated the scene in my mind as Mom shared it over and over again with friends and relatives. The doctor was cold, my parents stunned, and Donna seemingly unknowing. I did not know then the extent to which those events would not just touch but shape my own life.

Over the next three years Donna was in and out of hospitals, my parents filled with the urgency to save their oldest daughter, and I sometimes shuffled off to other households for varying amounts of time. My parents did their best to provide some kind of consistency for me, "the healthy one," but their focus, understandably, for the next thirty-three months was on my older sister.

Donna and I did love each other. I was more willing to show it publicly, much to my sister's embarrassment at times. We joined Blue Birds. Mom became a coleader. We went camping frequently. Donna and I were in a combination class together at one point. I was delighted to have her there until she started telling me to sit up and pay attention. She let me play with her Hot Wheels track and her electric train but I never could interest her in Barbies. We both enjoyed board games (even though we constantly accused each other of not playing fair) and we loved to draw. Her favorite subjects were horses and hospital things, mine were princesses and mice.

My mom learned how to administer chemotherapy so that Donna could come home. When she was in second grade, I in first, we attended a private school, I more regularly than she. Donna's hair began falling out as a result of the chemotherapy. Before returning to school, Mom took Donna shopping for wigs. They came home with one which very closely resembled Donna's own hair, dark brown with just the hint of curl at the end; the other was blond and curly, which Donna wore for fun. Most of the time, however, she wore stocking caps. Mom alerted the school staff that Donna would be wearing a wig to school. This wasn't something I had a problem with until my teacher gathered us into our reading circle and told the whole class that my sister would be returning to school wearing a wig. I was embarrassed and just a little angry. The other kids didn't need to know this personal stuff. She looked just like any other kid. Additionally, it invoked teasing and mumbled comments which, I am convinced, would not have occurred otherwise.

Unfortunately, Donna was not always able to stay home. Mom says she thanks God that he made me so self-entertaining and easygoing. I suppose it made it easier that I didn't fuss about where I would be staying, although I know she still feels guilty about having had to leave me in the care of others so often and sometimes for so long.

I never lacked love, not just from extended-family members but from townspeople as well. I knew I was welcome in whichever household I found myself, be it 5:30 A.M. in the morning at the Lecairs when Dad left for work (he and I stayed at home alone for a while when Mom was living at Children's Hospital at Stanford), or bedding down for the night at 8:30 P.M. at the Rosses. People went out of their way to prepare rooms for me, fix special meals, find things I might like to play with, take me out for ice cream. No, I never lacked love or attention, but I did miss my family. I felt that their lives were continuing without me.

When they went to Texas, I didn't understand why I couldn't go. Grammy went; why not me? When they moved Grandpa's trailer to Stanford, why couldn't I stay there, too? When my aunt went down during the final days of my sister's life, why wasn't I allowed to be there? She was my only sister, my comrade, my idol. Why was I being kept from her? Why didn't my parents want me around?

Each time we were reunited, I had had life experiences in which my parents had had no part, and vice versa. And it wasn't simply a matter of geography; their experiences went beyond anything I could imagine. Donna and I were growing further and further apart during the later stages of her illness. Additionally, I didn't understand why she didn't seem as excited to see me as I was to see her. I know why now, but I didn't understand it then. She was naturally less demonstrative than I was, and she didn't feel well most of the time.

I developed a whole slew of imaginary friends, most based on the characters from the Speed Racer or Kimba cartoons. I wrote them letters, held conversations with them, took them with me wherever I went. I even had an imaginary pet elephant in the backyard. All were attempts, I suppose, to provide for myself a constantly stable circle of "family" whose focus was solely on me.

After Donna's death, Mom, Dad, and I returned home to a houseful of people. I remember Dad gathering us all in the bedroom. I can't remember what was said, but I remember my dad crying. Later, as we viewed Donna's body in the casket, I remember her looking peaceful in her pink dress, holding a rosary which a nun had given her (even though we are not Catholic, we worship the same God). She seemed only to be asleep. Armed with that memory coupled with the term *passed away*, I quickly fell into a state of denial which lasted a little over four years.

I began having dreams in which I visited Donna in her hole in the wall (crypt in the mausoleum), easily accessible in my subconscious since my parents had not had her body buried in the ground. We would talk, watch TV, share french fries. Everything was fine, unless I asked her about being dead. Then her eyes rolled back into her head and her image started fading. I vowed never to bring up the subject again.

When a friend of a friend asked me one time while we played if I was the one whose sister had died, I replied with a panicked "No!" My friend assured her I was one and the same. The new girl wanted to know why, then, I had denied it. I let her know that my sister wasn't dead.

"Then what is she?" she asked me.

"Donna passed away," I announced triumphantly, knowing secretly in my heart that if she had passed away then she should be coming back. I just had to keep waiting.

And wait I did. Sometimes at night, after particularly rough days, I cried, and in my tears I would admit to missing Donna and wish her back home, which I could do without compromising my faith in her return. When I prayed I often gave God messages for Donna. Whether or not she got them I won't know until I join the throngs in heaven.

The next year was rough, because my parents were grieving, and I, too, felt empty even though I had not yet begun to grieve. My parents were concerned about raising me as an only child, but they couldn't decide whether to adopt or have another child. Just about the time they had decided to adopt, Mom became pregnant. This led to another stressful year. And just as I was not present at Donna's death, I was not present at Dayna's birth (although I did get to pick her name). Passively I added this to my stack of what I thought was evidence that my parents didn't want me around, that I was in the way.

Donna's death occurred just before I entered third grade. In fifth grade two sisters, Sherry and Linda Good, entered the school I attended. Sherry, like me, was chunky and in fifth grade. Linda was slender and in sixth. Both girls had dark brown hair and were thirteen months apart, just like Donna and me. Additionally, their mom was pregnant with a baby girl born months after Dayna. We all became part of a close-knit circle of friends.

The gang of us often got together for slumber(less) parties. Once in seventh grade, however, I asked my mom if just Sherry and Linda could spend the night. Of course they could, so they did. The next morning the two sisters started arguing, which they sometimes did at school. But this time it was in my own home. My heart broke. I was convinced that if one knew she might lose the other, they would never treat each other like that. And I could do nothing to squelch the disagreement.

Watching them glare and spit words at each other, I realized, after four long years, not only was Donna not around for me to argue with, she wasn't around for me to love, nor would she be returning. Her body lay decaying in the casket, her spirit hopefully relieved and rejoicing in heaven. I retreated to my bedroom and burst into tears, crying silently in an attempt to hide my pain.

Eventually, my mom started looking for me and found me sitting on the edge of my bed, my sinuses clogged, my eyes swollen, my cheeks, hands, and forearms slick with tears. Sitting next to me and putting her arm around my shoulders, she asked what was wrong. I couldn't answer. She then asked specifically if it was because Sherry and Linda were fighting. I nodded emphatically and managed to blurt out between two gasps, "I miss Donna!" Mom all but gathered me into her lap and rocked me for what seemed to be an eternity. It must have been painful for her as well. But it was needed, long overdue pain on my part. It was the beginning of the road to reality and acceptance.

I have sometimes found it difficult to get close to people for long periods of time since then. I would rather let them drift away after about five years or so. That way if they don't die, I can get back in touch with them and hopefully we can pick up right where we left off. Or if they do happen to die, I will have the memories and have already started the separation process. A great defense mechanism, but not very socially acceptable, that sometimes makes me downright lonely. But I never want to hurt like that again! I have encountered several deaths since then, many of them extended-family members and close family friends, but none as difficult as the death of my sister. As I grow older, though, I'm beginning to feel braver about taking risks, letting myself be more vulnerable, trusting other people with my emotions.

As Kübler-Ross will tell you, there are many steps to grief. The first, which I mastered, is denial. Somewhere between denial and acceptance is anger. And I experienced anger. I was angry at my parents for making the decision to turn off Donna's life support. I was angry at my aunt for not letting me go with her on that last trip to be with Donna. I was angry with my uncle for telling me my sister had died. I was angry at Dayna for reminding people so much of Donna. And I was angry at the kid in ninth grade who, after school one day, wished his sister was dead. Unbeknown to that poor, unsuspecting adolescent, he had just provided the break in the levy which contained my anger. The room fell silent as I laid into him loud and long about the pain of losing a sibling.

I am no longer angry. I have, indeed, accepted my sister's death. This same sentiment can be applied to my parents' divorce, as well. I have wondered, however, to what purpose God allowed all of this to transpire, especially since he promises in Romans 8:28 that for those who seek him all things will work together for good. I think I may have found at least part of the answer these last two years in my opportunity to deal with children in my classroom, some of whom have lost family members to divorce, drugs, and violence of many kinds. I think I may also have found the purpose in understanding a young, hurting, angry fifth grader who lost his older brother a few years ago to a terminal disease. I truly know how he feels.

Diana Matlock, schoolteacher, age twenty-six
September 1991

171

A Father's Grief
(This was read at Donna's funeral.)

I once was talking with a young priest who commented, "Parents question the death of a child, when actually the 'why' should be asked at birth." I dismissed his remark as lofty, ambiguous theology. However, his words returned to me, and as I considered them, I came to understand the harsh reality they contained.

Homo sapiens is Latin for "wise man." Granted, this assertion is open to debate, but there are characteristics that distinguish man from other forms of life: a mind that allows qualitative judgment based on intangibles; a soul that demands the worship of God in some manner; and a sex drive that is keyed to emotional involvement rather than triggered by a desire to continue the species.

We love and we have children, but the child is the result rather than the purpose of our love. If procreation were the main purpose of love, I doubt that many people would go through the trials of courtship and marriage. But we do, and we enter into relationships that we expect to last a lifetime. We expect, as does society, that children will result from this relationship. (I am generalizing, knowing that there is always the exception.) We accept the birth of our children as a matter of course. We love our children. We are proud. We carry their pictures in our pockets. Our friends are kept posted on their intellectual, physical, and social development. The children exist, become a part of our lifestyle, and our life continues on.

The Bible tells us that "for everything there is a season, a time to live and a time to die," and then reminds us that "it is appointed unto man once to die." If our child dies, we question God's judgment, berate his mercy, and deny his love. When we stop to think, we realize that we bring our child into existence through love with full knowledge that the eventual termination of that life is inevitable. Yet when God decrees that the life is to end, we tend to react with bitterness and rebellion. We create life without a second thought when we should be thinking, Why did God allow us to have this child? What are we to learn from this child? What is the child to learn from us? What paths are to be followed to fulfill God's expectations?

We have our child. We try to raise her to be an individual possessing all of our good qualities and none of the bad. We want her to grow up smarter, richer, handsomer, and better adjusted than we are. We struggle, worry, persevere, and love this child without acknowledging that she is "our" child only because of God's permission.

Since we know full well that every birth will ultimately result in death, it is futile to curse the inevitable. Death is preordained, and nothing has ever prevented it. If we must curse, let us not curse God for the death but ourselves for the birth. If we cannot accept God's decision, then we should studiously avoid any situation where his decision can affect us. We know, whether we admit it or not, that when we have a child, at some time in some way we will lose that child.

Since I knowingly and willingly helped to create a life, I should not complain when that life ends. It will hurt terribly, my heart will ache, my eyes will be filled with tears. The loneliness of separation from my child will seem overwhelming, but I cannot curse God for fulfilling his appointed scheme. In spite of the pain, I will thank God for the joy that my child has brought me, and I am grateful to him for allowing me to share in the brief life of his miracle—my child.

A Father's Epilogue

It has been eighteen years since I wrote these words and at least ten years since I last read them; years to come to terms with the statements "Time heals" or "It gets easier with time." Both are wrong. Time does not heal. I heal. By honestly feeling and acknowledging the grief, the pain, the loneliness, I am healing. It does not get easier with time. At times the anguish and grief of my child's dying is as fresh and as deep as it was eighteen years ago. What has happened with the passage of the years is that it gets hard less often. As time passed, I discovered that it had been an hour, a day, a week, since I had last thought of my child. I also discovered that this was all right. The memory of my child didn't die, nor disappear, nor even diminish for want of my constant attention.

There have been many changes during these intervening years, changes that have been, in their own way, as painful or significant and life altering as the death of my child. However, in rereading my words, I find one constant. I still thank God for allowing me to share in the brief life of this miracle—my child, my daughter Donna.

Don Matlock
September 1991

This poem by Edgar A. Guest was printed in the bulletin for Donna's memorial service.

To All Parents

"I'll lend you for a little time a child of mine," He said.
"For you to love him while he lives and mourn for when
   he's dead.
It may be six or seven years, or twenty-two or three,
But will you, till I call him back, take care of him for
   Me?
He'll bring his charms to gladden you, and should his
   stay be brief,
You'll have his lovely memories as solace for your grief.
I cannot promise he will stay, since all from earth return.
But there are lessons taught down there I want this child
   to learn.
I've looked the wide world over in my search for teach-
   ers true,
And from the throngs that crowd life's lanes I have
   selected you.
Now will you give him all your love, nor think the labor
   vain,
Nor hate Me when I come to call to take him back again?

"I fancied that I heard them say, 'Dear Lord, Thy will
   be done!
For all the joy Thy child shall bring, the risk of grief
   we'll run.
We'll shelter him with tenderness, we'll love him while
   we may.
And for the happiness we've known, forever grateful
   stay;

175

But should the angels call for him much sooner than
  we've planned
We'll brave the bitter grief that comes and try to understand.'"

Now imagine, if Donna could have written her story for us, what she would have said.

14

A Final Note to Helpers

Helpers walk a fine line. They are aware that, having worked with the dying child and family, they will need to mourn, too. But they should not become so involved with the family, nor should their own grief become so intense that they can no longer help.

However, I don't think keeping a safe, objective distance is the answer either. Helpers must sincerely feel the grief of those they help, but they should also be aware of their limitations. They need a network of other Christian helpers to support them through their own grief and warn them when they enter the emotional danger zones of getting too close to the situation. Helpers need to remember their own healthy families and friends who need them to care for them, enjoy life, and laugh with them today.

Helpers never can assume that their job is over and they can go on. They should stay in touch with grievers indefinitely. Helping and loving hurting people are lifetime missions. Jesus asked his disciple to care for and support Mary—for a week? for a month? for the first year? No, for her lifetime.

It is possible that some grieving families will cut off their relationships with you because you are a too painful reminder of their sad journeys. But that is their choice. You can lovingly contact them occasionally while respecting their boundaries.

Tools for the Helper

This book was written for helpers, but sections of it, especially family stories and Scripture references, are appropriate to share with grievers at the right time. Your other responsibility is to become familiar with information resources. This is the practical side of helping. Part 4 of this book contains the following:

1. a resource list of health-care organizations. Contact specific organizations to obtain technical information on individual diseases (e.g., cancer, cystic fibrosis). You should be knowledgeable about the diseases of the children you work with.
2. a resource list of support organizations. Become familiar with these groups to be able to recommend them to the dying and bereaved. Contact your local chapters.

3. a bibliography of books and other resources on hospitalization, therapy, death, and grief to further your knowledge in these fields.
4. a bibliography of children's books on hospitalization and death to be used with patients. You may want to begin developing your own library.

Becoming knowledgeable about this field will help you to be a better helper. Also contact local hospitals to learn about their program offerings.

God's Encouragement for Grievers and Helpers

Helpers are links in God's chain of comfort. They help the parents help their child die. They hold the parents as they grieve, and in time they will help other suffering parents. God is creating gold in each of us. He deeply loves the children whom he takes home early. He will never abandon us, no matter how hot the fire or how deep the pain.

> Should you pass through the sea, I will be with you;
> or through rivers, they will not swallow you up.
> Should you walk through fire, you will not be scorched
> and the flames will not burn you.
> For I am Yahweh your God,
> the Holy One of Israel, your saviour.
> (Isa. 43:2–3 JB)

> If I go eastward, he is not there;
> or westward—still I cannot see him.
> If I seek him in the north, he is not to be found,
> invisible still when I turn to the south.
> And yet he knows of every step I take!

179

Let him test me in the crucible: I shall come out pure gold.

(Job 23:8–10 JB)

As you walk through the fire of helping, bearing the burden of grief, you, too, will come out pure gold. May God go with you on your difficult and privileged journey.

PART 4

Children's Health-Care Resources

Health-Care Organizations

American Art Therapy Association, 1202 Allanson Rd., Mundelein, IL 60060

American Cancer Society, 1599 Clifton Rd., N.E., Atlanta, GA 30329

American Dance Therapy Association, 2000 Century Plaza, #108, Columbia, MD 21044

American Heart Association, 7320 Greenville Avenue, Dallas, TX 75231

American Juvenile Arthritis Organization, 1314 Spring St., N.W., Atlanta, GA 30309

Association for Brain Tumor Research, 3725 N. Talman Ave., Chicago, IL 60618

Association for the Care of Children's Health (ACCH), 7910 Woodmont Ave., Ste. 300, Bethesda, MD 20814-3015

Publishes: *Child Health Care*

Sub-organizations: Child Life Council

ACCH Network: Chronic Illness and Handicapping Conditions

For a comprehensive catalog of pediatric hospitalization resources and bibliographies, write to ACCH for their catalog.

Asthma and Allergy Association, 1717 Massachusetts Ave., Ste. 305, Washington, D.C. 20036

Cancer Information Service, 9000 Rockville Pike, Ste. 340, Bethesda, MD 20892 (800) 4-CANCER

Cystic Fibrosis Foundation, 6931 Arlington Rd., #200, Bethesda, MD 20814

Juvenile Diabetes Foundation, 432 Park Ave. S., New York, NY 10010

Leukemia Society of America, Inc., National Headquarters, 733 3rd Ave., New York, NY 10017

Mothers of AIDS Patients, P. O. Box 3132, San Diego, CA 92103

National AIDS Clearinghouse, P. O. Box 6003, Rockville, MD 20850 1-800-458-5231

National AIDS Hotline, ASHA, P. O. Box 13827, Research Triangle Park, NC 27709. 1-800-342-2437

National Association for Music Therapy, 505 11th Street, S.E., Washington, D.C. 20003

National Burn Victim Foundation, 308 Main St., Orange, NJ 07050

National Hemophilia Foundation, 110 Green St., #406, New York, NY 10012

National Kidney Foundation, 30 E. 33rd St., Ste. 1100, New York, NY 10016

National Association for Sickle Cell Disease, Inc., 3345 Wilshire Boulevard, Suite 1106, Los Angeles, CA 90010

Osteogenesis Imperfecta Foundation, Inc., P. O. Box 14807, Clearwater, FL 34629

Pediatric AIDS Foundation, 2407 Wilshire Boulevard, Ste. 613, Santa Monica, CA 90403

Pediatric Projects, Inc., P. O. Box 1880, Santa Monica, CA 90406-9920

Spina Bifida Association of America, 1700 Rockville Pike, #250, Rockville, MD 20852

Illness and Grief Support Organizations

Bereaved Parents, P. O. Box 3147, Scottsdale, AZ 85271

The Candlelighters Childhood Cancer Foundation, 1312 18th St., N.W., Washington, D.C. 20036

Children's Hospice International, CHI, 501 Slater's Lane #207, Alexandria, VA 22314

The Compassionate Friends, P. O. Box 3696, Oak Brook, IL 60522-3696

Make-A-Wish Foundation® of America, 2600 N. Central Ave., Ste. 936, Phoenix, AZ 85004 (602) 240-6600; (800) 722-WISH

Make Today Count, 101 1/2 S. Union St., Alexandria, VA 22314

The National Hospice Organization, 1901 N. Moore St., #901, Arlington, VA 22209

National Sudden Infant Death Syndrome Foundation, 10500 Little Patuxent Pkwy #420, Columbia, MD 21044

Parents of Murdered Children, 100 E. 8th St., B-14, Cincinnati, OH 45202

Pregnancy and Infant Loss Center, 1421 E. Wayzata Boulevard, #40, Wayzata, MN 55391

Ronald McDonald Houses, Children's Oncology Services, Inc., 500 N. Michigan Avenue, Chicago, IL 60611

Seasons: Suicide Bereavement, P. O. Box 187, Park City, UT 84060

The Ultimate Rejection - newsletter on suicide from: Suicide Prevention Center, Inc., 184 Salem Avenue, Dayton, OH 45406

Therapy Techniques for Hospitalized Children

Adams, M. A. "A Hospital Play Program: Helping Children with Serious Illness." *American Journal of Orthopsychiatry* 46:1976:416–425.

Akins and Mace. *The Hospitalized Child: Psychosocial Issues*. Bibliography, New York, 1981.

Anderson, Peggy. *Children's Hospital*. New York: Harper and Row, 1985.

Anthony and Kiupernik. *The Child in His Family: The Impact of Disease and Death.* New York: J. Wiley and Sons, 1973.

Azarnoff, Pat. *Medically Oriented Play for Children in Health Care*. Santa Monica: Pediatric Projects, 1986.

Azarnoff, Pat, and Sharon Flegal. *A Pediatric Play Program*. Springfield, Ill.: Thomas, 1975.

Azarnoff, Pat, ed. *Preparation of Young Healthy Children for Possible Hospitalization: The Issues.* Santa Monica: Pediatric Projects, Inc., 1983.

Belmont, H. "Hospitalization and Its Effect Upon the Total Child." *Clinical Pediatrics* 9 (1970): 472–483.

Bergman, T. *Children in the Hospital*. New York: International University Press, 1965.

Bilotti, E. *Getting Children Home: Hospital to Community*. Washington, D.C.: Georgetown University Child Development Center, 1984.

Bombeck, Erma, *I Want to Grow Hair, I Want to Grow Up, I Want to Go to Boise: Children Surviving Cancer*. New York: Harper and Row, 1989.

Clarke, H., and G. Robinson, eds. *The Hospital Care of Children*. New York: Oxford University Press, 1980.

Covell, M. *The Home Alternative to Hospitals and Nursing Homes*. New York: Rawson Associates, 1983.

Debuskey, M. *The Chronically Ill Child and His Family*. Springfield, Ill.: Charles C. Thomas Company, 1970.

Family-Centered Care Issue, *Children's Health Care* 17, (Fall 1988).

Fassler, J. *Helping Children Cope: Managing Stress Through Books and Stories*. New York: Free Press, 1978.

Gellert, E. *Psychosocial Aspects of Pediatric Care*. New York: Grune and Stratton, 1978.

Haller, J. ed. *The Hospitalized Child and His Family*. Baltimore: Johns Hopkins Press, 1967.

Hardgrove, C. *Parents and Children in the Hospital*. Boston: Little, Brown and Company, 1972.

Hofmann, Becker, Gabriel. *The Hospitalized Adolescent*. New York: Free Press, 1976.

Klinzing, D. R., and D. G. Klinzing. *The Hospitalized Child: Communication Techniques for Health Personnel*. Englewood Cliffs, N.J.: Prentice-Hall, 1977.

Lindheim, R., H. H. Glaser, and C. Coffin. *Changing Hospital Environments for Children*. Cambridge: Harvard University Press, 1972.

Lindquist, Ivonney. *Therapy Through Play*. London: Arlington Books, 1977.

Linn, S. "Puppet Therapy in Hospitals: Helping Children Cope." *Journal of the American Medical Women's Association* 33(2). (1978).

McCollum, A. *The Chronically Ill Child*. New Haven: Yale University Press, 1981.

Nierenberg, Judith, and Florence Janovic. *The Hospital Experience: A Guide for Patients and Their Families*. Berkeley Books, 1985.

Oremland, E. and J. Oremland. *The Effects of Hospitalization on Children: Models for Their Care*. Evanston, Ill. Charles C. Thomas, 1973.

Petrillo, M., and S. Sanger. *The Emotional Care of Hospitalized Children*. Philadelphia: J. B. Lippincott, 1980.

Philpott, A. R., ed. *Puppets and Therapy*. Boston: Plays, 1977.

Plank, E. *Working With Children in Hospitals*. Chicago: Press of Case Western Reserve University, 1962.

Play Therapy Issue, *Children's Health Care* 17 (Fall 1988).

Thompson, R. *Psychosocial Research on Pediatric Hospitalization*. Springfield, Ill.: Charles C. Thomas, 1985.

Thompson, Richard, and Gene Stanford. *Child Life in Hospitals: Theory and Practice.* Evanston, Ill.: Charles C. Thomas, 1981.

Travis, Georgia. *Chronic Illness in Children: Its Impact on Child and Family*. Stanford, Calif.: Stanford University Press, 1976.

The Use of Creative Arts in Therapy. Washington, D.C.: American Psychiatric Association, 1980.

Vernon, D. *The Psychological Responses of Children to Hospitalization and Illness*. Evanston, Ill.: Charles C. Thomas, 1965.

Walsh, S. "Puppet Helpers." *Pediatric Nursing* 6(2) (1980).

Books

Death and Grief

Anderson, Ray S. *Theology, Death and Dying*. New York: Basil Blackwell, 1986.

Arterburn, Jerry. *How Will I Tell My Mother?* Nashville: Thomas Nelson Publishers, 1988.

Barckley, V. "Grief, A Part of Living." American Cancer Society, 1968.

Bayly, J. *Ministering to the Terminally Ill*. Elgin, Ill.: David C. Cook.

Biregert, John E. *When Death Has Touched Your Life*. New York: The Pilgrim Press, 1981.

Bloom, Lois A. *Mourning After Suicide*. New York: The Pilgrim Press, 1986.

Bozarth-Campbell, Alla. *Life Is Goodbye—Life Is Hello*. Minneapolis: CompCare Publications, 1982.

Buckingham, Robert W. *The Complete Hospice Guide*. New York: Harper and Row, 1983.

Burnham, Betsy. *When Your Friend Is Dying*. Grand Rapids: Chosen Books, 1982.

Cain, Albert C., ed. *Survivors of Suicide*. Springfield, Ill.: Charles C. Thomas, 1972.

Callari, Elizabeth S. *A Gentle Death: Personal Caregiving to the Terminally Ill*. Greensboro, N.C.: Tudor Publishers, Inc., 1986.

Colgrove, Melba, Harold H. Bloomfield, and Peter McWilliams. *How to Survive the Loss of a Love*. New York: Bantam Books, 1976.

Cousins, Norman. *Anatomy of an Illness*. New York: Bantam Books, 1979.

Davidson, Glen. *Living with Dying*. Minneapolis: Augsburg Publishing House, 1975.

Decker, Bea. *After the Flowers Have Gone*. Grand Rapids: Zondervan Publishing House, 1973.

Deford, F. *Alex: The Life of a Child*. New York: Viking Press, 1983.

Dobihal, Edward F., Jr., and Charles William Stewart. *When a Friend is Dying—A Guide to Caring for the Terminally Ill and Bereaved*. Nashville: Abingdon Press, 1984.

Duda, Deborah. *Coming Home*. Santa Fe: John Muir Publications Co., 1984.

Elliott, Elisabeth. *Facing the Death of a Loved One*. Westchester, Ill.: Good News Publishers, 1973. (Booklet)

Griffith, William, H. *Confronting Death*. Valley Forge, Penn.: Judson Press, 1977.

Grollman, Earl A. *What Helped Me When My Loved One Died*. Boston: Beacon Press, 1981.

Grollman, Earl A. *When Your Loved One is Dying*. Boston: Beacon Press, 1980.

Hamilton, Michael P., and Helen F. Reid, eds. *A Hospice Handbook*. Grand Rapids: Wm. B. Eerdmans Publishing Co., 1980.

Hayford, Jack W., Jr. *I'll Hold You in Heaven*. Ventura, Calif.: Regal Books, 1986.

Hendin, David. *Death as a Fact of Life*. New York: W. W. Norton and Company, 1984.

Hubbard, David Allen. *Why Do I Have to Die?* Glendale, Calif.: Regal Books, 1978.

Ivan, L., and M. Melrose. *The Way We Die*. West Sussex, United Kingdom: Angel Press, 1986.

Jackson, E. *Understanding Grief*. New York: Abingdon Press.

Jackson, Edgar N. *The Many Faces of Grief*. Nashville: Abingdon Press, 1972.

Jensen, Amy. *Healing Grief*. Medic Publishing Co., 1980.

Klagsbrun, Francine. *Too Young to Die: Youth and Suicide*. Boston: Houghton Mifflin, 1984.

Kopp, Ruth. *When Someone You Love Is Dying—A Handbook for Counselors and Those Who Care*. Grand Rapids: Zondervan Publishing House, 1980.

Kreeft, P. J. *Love Is Stronger Than Death*. New York: Harper and Row, 1979.

Kreis, Bernadine, and Alice Pattie. *Up From Grief: Patterns of Recovery*. Minneapolis: The Seabury Press, 1969.

Kubler-Ross, Elisabeth. *Death: The Final Stage of Growth*. Englewood Cliffs, N.J.: Prentice-Hall, 1975.

Kubler-Ross, Elisabeth. *On Death and Dying*. Chicago: University of Chicago Press, 1968.

Kubler-Ross, Elisabeth. *Questions and Answers on Death and Dying*. New York: The Macmillan Publishing Co., 1974.

Kubler-Ross, Elisabeth, and Mel Warslow. *To Live Until We Say Good-Bye*. Englewood Cliffs, N.J.: Prentice-Hall, 1978.

Kuenning, Delores. *Helping People Through Grief*. Minneapolis: Bethany House, 1987.

Kuklin, Susan. *Fighting Back: What Some People Are Doing About AIDS*. New York: Putnam, 1988.

Lerner, Ethan A. *Understanding AIDS*. Minneapolis: Lerner, 1987.

Lewis, C. S. *A Grief Observed*. New York: Bantam Books, 1961.

Magee, Doug. *What Murder Leaves Behind: The Victim's Family*. New York: Dodd, Mead and Company.

Martinson, Ida M., ed. *Home Care for the Dying Child: Professional and Family Perspectives*. New York: Appleton-Century Crofts, 1976.

Mays, L. H. "Cancer Management: The Role of the Clergy." Proceedings of the American Cancer Society, 1978.

Mitchell, Kenneth R., and Herbert Anderson. *All Our Losses, All Our Griefs: Resources for Pastoral Care*. Philadelphia: The Westminster Press, 1983.

Moldow, D. Gary, and Ida M. Martinson. *Home Care for Seriously Ill Children: A Manual for Parents*. Alexandria, Va.: Children's Hospice, 1984.

Moster, Mary Beth. *Living with Cancer*. Wheaton: Tyndale House, 1979.

Nourse, Alan. *AIDS*. New York: Franklin Watts, 1986.

Rando, Therese A. *Grief, Dying, and Death*. Champaign, Ill.: Research Press Company, 1984.

Rank, Maureen. *Free to Grieve: Coping with the Trauma of Miscarriage*. Minneapolis: Bethany House Publishers, 1985.

Ross, Eleanora. *After Suicide: A Unique Grief Process*. Iowa City: Ray of Hope, Inc., 1986.

Scherzer, C. *Ministering to the Dying*. New York: Prentice-Hall.

Shepard, Martin. *Someone You Love Is Dying*. New York: Harmony Books, 1975.

Soulen, R. N. *Care for the Dying*. Atlanta: John Knox Press, 1978.

Swartz, Penny Siegel. *The Sky Is Bluer Now: Thoughts on Living with Cancer*. Self-Help Center, 1600 Dodge Avenue, Ste. S 122, Evanston, IL 60201.

Switzer, David. *Dynamics of Grief*. Nashville: Abingdon Press, 1970.

Switzer, David. *The Minister as Crisis Counselor*. Nashville: Abingdon Press, 1974.

Tengborn, Mildred. *Grief for a Season*. Minneapolis: Bethany House, 1973.

Towns, James E. *Growing Through Grief*. Anderson, Ind.: Warner Press, Inc., 1984.

Vail, Elaine. *A Personal Guide to Living with Loss*. New York: John Wiley and Sons, Inc., 1982.

Van Auken, S. *A Severe Mercy*. San Francisco: Harper and Row, 1977.

Verwoerdt, A. *Communication with the Fatally Ill*. American Cancer Society, 1965.

Westberg, Granger E. *Good Grief*. Minneapolis: Fortress Press, 1962.

Westberg, G. *Minister and Doctor Meet*. New York: Harper and Row.

Wiersbe, Warren W. *Why Us? When Bad Things Happen to God's People*. Old Tappan, N. J.: Fleming H. Revell Company, 1984.

Williams, D. D. *The Minister and the Care of Souls*. Harper's Ministers, 1977.

Worden, William J. *Grief Counseling and Grief Therapy: A Handbook for the Mental Health Practitioner*. New York: Springer Publishing Company, 1982.

Wrobleski, Adrina. *Suicide: Questions and Answers; Suicide: The Danger Signs*; and *Suicide: Your Child Has Died—For All Parents*. 5124 Grove Street, Minneapolis, MN.

Zanca, Kenneth J. *Mourning: The Healing Journey*. Locust Valley, N.Y.: Living Flame Press, 1980.

Children and Death

Anthony, Sylvia. *The Discovery of Death in Childhood and After*. England: Penguin Books, 1973.

Anthony-Koupernick. *The Child and His Family: Impact of Disease and Death*. New York: J. Wiley and Sons, 1973.

Arnold, Joan H., and Pénelope R. Buschmann-Gemma. *A Child Dies: A Portrait of Family Grief*. Gaithersburg, Md.: Aspen Publishing, 1983.

Adams and Deveau. *Coping With Childhood Cancer*. Reston, Va.: Reston Publishers, 1984.

Bluebond-Langer, Myra. *The Private Worlds of Dying Children*. Princeton, N.J.: Princeton University Press, 1978.

Buckingham, Robert W. *A Special Kind of Love—Care of the Dying Child*. New York: The Continuum Publishing Co., 1983.

Church, Martha Jo, Helene Chazin, and Faith Ewald. *When a Baby Dies*. The Compassionate Friends, P. O. Box 3696, Oak Brook, IL 60522-3696.

Cook, S. *Children and Dying*. New York: Health Sciences, 1973.

DeFrain, John, Jacque Taylor, and Linda Ernst. *Coping with Sudden Infant Death*, Lexington, Mass.: Lexington Books, 1982.

DeFrain, John D., Leona Martens, Jan Stork, and Warren Stork, *Stillborn: The Invisible Death*. D. C. Heath and Company, Lexington Books, 1986.

Dickens, M. *Miracles of Courage*. New York: Dodd, Mead and Co., 1985.

Dodd, Robert V. *Helping Children Cope with Death*. Scottdale, Penn.: Herald Press, 1984.

Donnelly, Katharine F. *Recovering from the Loss of a Child*. New York: Macmillan Publishing, 1982.

Easson, William M. *The Dying Child*. Springfield, Ill.: Charles C. Thomas, 1970.

Frantz, T. *When Your Child Has a Life-Threatening Illness*. ACCH, 1983.

Gaffney, D.A. *The Seasons of Grief: Helping Children Grow Through Loss*. New York: New American Library, Dutton, 1988.

Grollman, Earl A., ed. *Explaining Death to Children*. Boston: Beacon Press, 1967.

Grollman, Earl, *Talking About Death: A Dialogue Between Parent and Child*. Boston: Beacon Press, 1970.

Harberts, G. M. *Interpreting Death to Children*. Christian Education Department of the San Marino Community Church, 1956.

Hyde, *Cancer in the Young: A Sense of Hope*. Philadelphia: Westminster Press, 1985.

Ilse, Sherokee. *Empty Arms: Coping After Miscarriage, Stillbirth and Infant Death*. The Compassionate Friends.

Jackson, Edgar N. *Telling a Child About Death.* New York: Channel Press, 1965.

Jewett, Claudia L. *Helping Children Cope with Separation and Loss*. Boston: Harvard Common Press, 1982.

Knapp, Ronald J. *Beyond Endurance: When a Child Dies*. New York: Schocken Books, 1986.

La Tour, Kathy. *For Those Who Live: Helping Children Cope with the Death of a Brother or Sister*. Write to Kathy La Tour, P. O. Box 141182, Dallas, TX 75214.

Limbo, Rana K., and Sara Rich Wheeler. *When a Baby Dies: A Handbook for Healing and Helping*. 1986. Resolve Through Sharing, LaCrosse Lutheran Hospital, 1910 South Avenue, La Crosse, WI 54601.

Martinson, Ida M. *Home Care for the Dying Child*. Appleton-Century Crofts, 1976.

Miles, Margaret Shandor. *The Grief of Parents . . . When a Child Dies*. Oak Brook, Ill.: The Compassionate Friends, 1978.

Moldow, D. Gay, and Ida M. Martinson. *Home Care for Seriously Ill Children*. Alexandria, Va.: Children's Hospice International, 1984.

Osgood, Judy. *Meditations for Bereaved Parents*. The Compassionate Friends. Sunriver, Oreg.: Gilgal Publishing, 1984.

Rando, Therese A., ed. *Parental Loss of a Child*. Champaign, Ill.: Research Press Co., 1986.

Reed, Elizabeth L. *Helping Children with the Mystery of Death*. Nashville: Abingdon Press, 1970.

Rogers, Fred. *Talking with Young Children about Death*. NFDA Library of Publication, 11121 West Oklahoma Avenue, Milwaukee, WI 53227.

Rosen, Helen. *Unspoken Grief: Coping with Childhood Sibling Loss*. Rutgers, N.J.: Lexington Books, 1986.

Rudolph, Marguerita. *Should the Children Know?* New York: Schocken Books, Inc., 1978.

Sahler, O. J. Z. *The Child and Death*. C. V. Mosby, 1978.

Schaefer, Dan, and Christine Lyons. *How Do We Tell the Children: A Parents' Guide to Helping Children Understand and Cope When Someone Dies*. New York: Newmarket Press, 1986.

Schaltz, Bill. *Healing a Father's Grief*. The Compassionate Friends.

Schiff, Harriett S. *The Bereaved Parent*. Crown Publishers, 1977.

Spinetta, J. *Living With Childhood Cancer*. St. Louis: Mosby, 1981.

Stevenson, Nancy C., and Cary H. Straffon. *When Your Child Dies: Finding the Meaning in Mourning*. Lakewood, Ohio: Theo Publishing Co., 1981.

Thomas, J., ed. *Death and Dying in the Classroom*. Phoenix: Oryx Press, 1984.

U.S. Department of Health and Human Services. *Maintaining a Normal Life*. Proceedings of the Candlelighters Foundation Conference, 1980.

U.S. Department of Health, Education and Welfare. *Students with Cancer*. 1980.

Vogel, Linda Jane. *Helping a Child Understand Death*. Philadelphia: Fortress Press, 1975.

Vredevelt, Pam W. *Empty Arms: Emotional Support for Those Who Have Suffered Miscarriage or Stillbirth*. Portland, Oreg.: Multnomah Press, 1984.

Children's Books on Death

Adkins, M. *Orknon Was My Friend*. Hamilton, Ontario: Image, 1984.

Alex, Marlee and Ben, *Grandpa & Me—We Learn About Death*. Minneapolis: Bethany House, 1982.

Alsop, Stewart. *Stay of Execution*. Philadelphia: Lippincott Co., 1973.

American Cancer Society. *What Happened to You Happened to Me*. New York: American Cancer Society, 1984.

American Cancer Society. *When Your Brother or Sister Has Cancer*. New York: American Cancer Society, 1984.

Anders, R. *A Look at Death*. Minneapolis: Lerner, 1977.

Arnold, K. *Anna Joins In*. Nashville: Abingdon, 1983.

Bach, Alice. *Waiting for Johnny Miracle*. New York: Harper and Row, 1980.

Baker, L. *You and Leukemia: A Day at a Time*. Philadelphia: Saunders, 1978.

Barker, Peggy. *What Happened When Grandma Died?* St. Louis: Concordia Publishing House, 1984.

Bernstein, J., and S. Gullo. *When People Die*. 1977.

Bisignano, Judith. *Living with Death*. Kansas City, Mo.: 1985.

Blackburn, L. *Timothy Duck: The Story of the Death of a Friend*. Omaha: Centering Corporation, 1987.

Brady, M. *Please Remember Me*. New York: Archway, 1978.

Bruce, Shelley. *Tomorrow Is Today*. New York: Macmillan, 1983.

Bunting, E. *The Empty Window*. New York: Warner, 1980.

Burns, S. *Cancer: Understanding and Fighting It*. New York: Messner, 1982.

Buscaglia, Leo. *The Fall of Freddie the Leaf: A Story of Life for All Ages*. New York: Holt, Rinehart, and Winston, 1982.

Calvert, P. *The Stone Pony*. New York: Scribners, 1982.

Center for Attitudinal Healing. *There Is a Rainbow Behind Every Dark Cloud*. Millbrae, Calif.: Celestial Arts, 1979.

Center for Attitudinal Healing, G. Murray and G. Jampolsky. *Straight From the Siblings: Another Look at the Rainbow*. Millbrae, Calif.: Celestial Arts, 1983.

Cera, Mary Jane. *Living with Death*. Tucson: Kino Publications.

Cohn, Janice. *I Had a Friend Named Peter*. New York: William Morrow Co., 1987.

Cystic Fibrosis Foundation, *Living With Cystic Fibrosis: A Guide for Adolescents*. Rockville, Md.: Cystic Fibrosis Foundation, 1984.

Dixon, P. *May I Cross Your Golden River*. New York: Atheneum, 1975.

Dodge, Joyce. *"Mommy, What's AIDS?"* Wheaton: Tyndale House, 1989.

Dodge, Nancy C. *Thumpy's Story: A Story of Love and Grief Shared*. Springfield, Ill.: Prairie Lark Press, 1984.

Fassler, Joan. *My Grandpa Died Today*. New York: Behavorial Publications, Inc., 1971.

Fine, Judylaine. *Afraid to Ask: A Book for Families to Share About Cancer*. New York: Lothrop, Lee and Shepard, 1986.

Fox, R. *Angela Ambrosia*. New York: Knopf, 1979.

Frevert, P. *Patty Gets Well*. Mankato, Minn.: Creative Education, 1983.

Gravelle, Karen and John, Bertram. *Teenagers Face-to-Face With Cancer*. New York: Messner, 1986.

Gunther, John. *Death Be Not Proud*. New York: Harper and Row, 1971.

Haines, G. *Cancer*. New York: Franklin Watts, 1980.

Hazen, Barbara Shook. *Why Did Grandpa Die?* New York: Golden Books, 1985.

Herder, M. *The End Beginning.* Chorister Guild Letters, 1976.

Hickman, M. *Last Week My Brother Anthony Died.* Nashville: Abingdon, 1984.

Hughes, M. *Hunter in the Dark.* Paterson, N.J.: Atheneum, 1983.

Hyde, Margaret O., and Elizabeth Forsythe. *AIDS: What Does it Mean to You?* New York: Walker, 1986.

Hyde, Margaret O., and Lawrence E. Hyde. *Cancer in the Young: A Sense of Hope.* Philadelphia: Westminster, 1985.

Ipswitch, E. *Scott Was Here.* 1978.

Johnson, Jay, et. al. *Where's Jess?* Omaha: Centering Corporation, 1982.

Klein, Norma. *Sunshine.* New York: Avon, 1982.

Kopp, Ruth. *Where Has Grandpa Gone?* Grand Rapids: Zondervan Publishing House, 1983.

Kruckeberg, Carol. *What Was Good About Today.* Seattle: Madrona, 1984.

Lancaster, M. *Hang Tough.* North Canton, Ohio: Matthew Lancaster, 1983.

Lee, V. *The Magic Moth.* Burlington, Mass.: Houghton Mifflin, 1972.

Leukemia Society of America. *What It Is That I Have, Don't Want, Didn't Ask for, Can't Give Back, and How I Feel About It.* New York: Leukemia Society of America.

Linn, Erin. *Children Are Not Paper Dolls: A Visit with Bereaved Siblings.* Cary, Ill.: Linn Press, 1982.

Lowry, L. *A Summer to Die.* Burlington, MA: Houghton Mifflin, 1977.

Lund, Doris. *Eric.* New York: Dell, 1976.

McLendon, G. *My Brother Joey Dies.* 1982.

Mellonie, Bryan, and Robert Ingpen. *Lifetimes: The Beautiful Way to Explain Death to Children.* New York: Bantam, 1983.

Miller, Robyn. *Robyn's Book: Growing Up with Cystic Fibrosis.* New York: Scholastic, 1986.

Miner, J. *Mountain Fear: When a Brother Dies.* Mankato, Minn.: Crestwood, 1982.

Miner, J. *This Day is Mine: Living with Leukemia.* Mankato, Minn.: Crestwood, 1982.

Nathanson, Minna. *Candlelighters Childhood Cancer Foundation Bibliography and Resource Guide.* 1987.

National Cancer Institute. *Help Yourself—Tips for Teenagers with Cancer.* Bethesda, Md.: National Cancer Institute, 1983.

National Cancer Institute. *When Someone in Your Family Has Cancer.* Bethesda, Md.: National Cancer Institute, 1985.

Norris, Louanne. *An Oak Tree Dies and a Journey Begins.* New York: Crown Publishers, Inc., 1979..

Pendleton, E. *Too Old to Cry, Too Young to Die.* Nashville: Thomas Nelson, 1980.

Poole, V. *Thursday's Child.* Boston: Little, Brown, 1980.

Richter, Elizabeth. *Losing Someone You Love.* New York: Putnam, 1986.

Rofes, Eric, ed. *The Kids Book About Death and Dying.* Boston: Little, Brown, 1985.

Siegel, D. *Winners: Eight Special Young People.* New York: Messner, 1978.

Silverstein, Alvin, and Virginia B. Silverstein. *AIDS: Deadly Threat*. Hillside, N.J.: Enslow, 1986.

Simon, N., *We Remember Phillip*. Chicago: Albert Whitman, 1978.

Simonides, Carol. *I'll Never Walk Alone. The Inspiring Story of a Teenager's Struggle Against Cancer*. New York: Continuum, 1983.

Sims, Alicia. *Am I Still a Sister?* The Compassionate Friends.

Smith, Dora B. *A Taste of Blackberries*. New York: Harper, 1973.

Stein, S. *About Dying*. New York: Walker, 1984.

Strasser, Todd. *Friends Till the End*. New York: Dell, 1982.

Thomas, J.R. *Saying Good-Bye to Grandma*. New York: Clarion Books, 1988.

Vogel, I. *My Twin Sister Erika*. New York: Harper and Row, 1976.

Children and Hospitalization

Anderson, P. *The Operation*. ACCH, 1979.

Baznik, D. *Becky's Story*. Washington, D.C.: ACCH, 1981.

Bemelmans, L. *Madeline*. New York: Penguin, 1977.

Berger, K., R. Tidwell, and M. Haseltine. *A Visit to the Doctor*. 1978.

Biomedical Graphic Communications. *Stevie Has His Heart Repaired*. Atlanta: Pritchett and Hull Associates, 1979.

Biomedical Graphic Communications. *Stevie Has His Heart Examined*. Atlanta: Pritchett and Hull Associates, 1983.

Bock, G., and M. Hoff. eds. *Someone Special—How Mike Learns to Live with Kidney Disease*. Minneapolis: Minnesota Medical Foundation, 1981.

Bruna, D. *Miffy in the Hospital*. Los Angeles: Price/Stern/Sloan, 1984.

Chirinian, H. *Danny Goes to the Doctor*. Los Angeles: Price/Stern/Sloan, 1986.

Chirinian, H. *Henry Goes to the Hospital*. Los Angeles: Price/Stern/Sloan, 1986.

Coleman, William L. *My Hospital Book*. Minneapolis: Bethany House, 1981.

Elliott, Ingrid G. *Hospital Roadmap: A Book to Help Explain the Hospital Experience to Young Children*. Cambridge, Mass.: Resources for Children in Hospitals, 1984.

Family Communications, *Going to the Hospital*. Family Communications, 4802 Fifth Avenue, Pittsburgh, PA 15213, 1977.

Family Communications, *Having an Operation*. Family Communications, 4802 Fifth Avenue, Pittsburgh, PA 15213, 1978.

Gaes, J. *My Book for Kids with Cancer*. ACCH, 1987.

Hantzig, Deborah. *A Visit to the Sesame Street Hospital*. New York: Random House, 1985.

Hogan, Paula A., and Kirk Hogan. *The Hospital Scares Me*. Milwaukee: Raintree Publications, 1980.

Howe, Jane. *The Hospital Book*. New York: Crown, 1981.

Jones, P., *Living with Hemophilia*. Philadelphia: Davis, 1974.

Livingston, Carole, and Claire Ciliotta. *Why Am I Going to the Hospital?* Secaucus, N.J.: Lyle Stuart, 1981.

Perez, Carla, and Deborah Robison. *Your Turn, Doctor.* New York: Dial Press, 1984.

Phillips, J., J. Bowen, and A. Farris. *When You Visit the ICU.* Washington, D.C.: ACCH, 1982.

Phillips, J., J. Bowen, and A. Farris. *Your Heart Test.* Washington, D.C.: ACCH, 1983.

Reit, S. *Jenny's in the Hospital.* New York: Golden Book, 1984.

Reit, S. *Some Busy Hospital!* Racine, Wis.: Western, 1985.

Rey, H., and M. Rey. *Curious George Goes to the Hospital.* Boston: Houghton Mifflin, 1966.

Richter, E. *The Teenage Hospital Experience: You Can Handle It!* 1982.

Rockwell, Anne, and Harlow Rockwell. *Sick in Bed.* New York: Macmillan, 1982.

Rockwell, Anne. *The Emergency Room.* Macmillan, 1985.

Rockwell, H. *My Doctor.* New York: Macmillan, 1973.

Rogers, Fred. *Going to the Doctor.* New York: Putnam, 1986.

Scarry, Richard. *Richard Scarry's Nicky Goes to the Doctor.* Racine, Wis.: Western, 1978.

Shay, A. *What Happens When You Go to the Hospital.* Chicago: Reilly and Lee, 1969.

Singer, M. *It Can't Hurt Forever.* New York: Harper and Row, 1978.

Sobol, H. *Jonathan's Hospital Book.* Bialis Family Foundation, 1987.

Steedman, J. *Emergency Room: An ABC Tour.* 1974.

Stein, Sara B. *The Hospital Story.* New York: Walker, 1984.

Tamburine, J. *I Think I Will Go to the Hospital.* Nashville: Abingdon Press, 1965.

Tully, M. A., and M. Tully. *Heart Disease*. New York: Franklin Watts, 1980.

Ward, B. *Hospital*. Morristown, N. J.: Silver Burdett, 1978.

Warmbier, J., and E. Vassy. *Hospital Days, Treatment Ways*. Bethesda, Md.: National Cancer Center, 1982.

You're Gonna Do What? Little Rock, Ark.: Arkansas Children's Hospital, 1984. Booklet series on medical preparation.

Notes

Chapter 4

1. From the sermon, "Faith Revisited," by Steve Fretwell, June 26, 1988, Benicia First Baptist Church, Benicia, California.

Chapter 5

1. Thanks to Mike and Victoria Haskins for sharing their story.

Chapter 6

1. Thanks to dance therapists Lisa Curry and Lynn Koshland for these ideas.

Chapter 8

1. Thanks to Kathy and David Werum for telling of their experience and giving permission to print their journal writings.

Chapter 11

1. Thanks to Virginia and Ron Hiramatsu for telling of their experience.